Sexual Abuse of Children in the 1980's

Edited by Benjamin Schlesinger

# SEXUAL ABUSE of children in the 1980's

Ten Essays and an Annotated Bibliography

UNIVERSITY OF TORONTO PRESS
Toronto        Buffalo        London

© University of Toronto Press 1986
Toronto  Buffalo  London
Printed in Canada
ISBN 0-8020-6622-4

**Canadian Cataloguing in publication Data**

Main entry under title:
Sexual abuse of children in the 1980's
Includes index.
Bibliography: p.
ISBN 0-8020-6622-4
1. Child molesting.  I. Schlesinger, Benjamin, 1928-
HQ71.S38 1986        362.7'044        C86-093984-7

# CONTENTS

# PREFACE

The topic of sexual abuse of children has been in the fore-
front of American and Canadian society in the 1980's. In
1982, the University of Toronto Press published my book
Sexual Abuse of Children: A Resource Guide and Annotated
Bibliography. The book was an attempt to present the findings related to the topic up to 1980, and contained 180
items in the annotated bibliography. I was pleased by the
positive reception this effort had among the readers and
reviewers.

Since 1980, there have been many new studies, projects,
and reports on the topic. This new book contains ten papers
dealing with varied aspects related to sexual abuse of children. Of the eleven authors, nine are Canadians and two are
Americans. I am grateful for their permission and that of
their publishers to reprint their contributions. The papers
were originally published during the 1982-1985 period.

The topical annotated bibliography (1980-1985) contains
310 entries. I am sure that I have overlooked some entries
during that productive period. I have included only published articles, books, booklets, and reports primarily from
Canada and the United States.

The appendix contains a selected list of audio-visual resources, addresses of primary sources who distribute materials on the topic and an author's index.

I was able to produce this book only because of a grant
from the Child Abuse Prevention Program of the Ministry of
Community and Social Services of the Province of Ontario,
Canada. Sam Morreale, the director of the program was helpful in suggesting the direction of this volume.

I want to also thank my Dean, Dr. Ralph Garber for his
continued support, R.I.K. Davidson my editor at the
University of Toronto Press, and Gwen Peroni my typist, for

their part in this effort. Last but not least my wife
Rachel, and children, Avi, Leo, Esther and Michael stood by
me while I laboured at producing this book.

I would like to dedicate this book to the thousands of
persons who work with sexually abused children and their
families in the 1980's. I hope that their efforts will
reduce the incidence and frequency of sexual abuse.

Benjamin Schlesinger
Faculty of Social Work
University of Toronto
December 1985

*To the Reader*

The intent of the author in selecting articles was to
illustrate a cross-section of viewpoints. The views
expressed do not necessarily reflect those of the author nor
of the Ministry of Community and Social Services of Ontario.
Readers are encouraged to pursue the topics further through
their own reading and research.

Sexual Abuse of Children in the 1980's

1. FIFTY MYTHS AND FACTS ABOUT INCEST

LADA I. TAMARACK

These myths have been gathered from statements being made,
and from articles being distributed in Canada, written by
professionals who are considered knowledgeable on the subject. We are writing out of concern for precedents being set
which are damaging to incest survivors.

1. Myth  Some children lie.
   Fact   This is often the first defense that an attacker
          will use against a victim who has spoken. Children
          don't lie, and don't imagine the sexually explicit
          acts that they are describing. Although this myth
          is dying, people still find it difficult to be-
          lieve children when the family 'appears normal,'
          or when the rapes have been extensive, or when
          torture has been used. There is still a tendency
          to believe that 'it can't be true.' Confusion in a
          child should not be seen as lying. A defensive
          parent may want to grasp at some discrepancy in a
          child's story. Children must be given the time and
          encouragement to sort out what did happen from
          very natural fears arising from the rape itself,
          or from repeated threats often made by the at-
          tacker 'if she told.'

2. Myth  Children fantasize about incest. Every daughter
          has fantasies about a romantic relationship with
          her father. Every son imagines a romantic rela-
          tionship with his mother. Incest comes from an un-
          conscious oedipal wish.
   Fact   These myths originate in freudian thought, and may
          be confused with a child's wanting or needing love
          and caring. Unfortunately, Freud's theories on

incest continue to be taught as valid in Canadian universities. Within the past ten years his rationalizations about the overwhelming amount of incest becoming evident in the 1800's, have been recognized as a clever cover-up. Freud put the blame on children for what adults were imposing. What he was confronted with was father/daughter incest, and his fear of ostracization by his fellows for exposing what was taking place, caused him do develop his elaborate theories.

3. Myth   If the child has not been coerced, it is not incest.
   Fact   Incest takes many forms, from violent rape including penetration, to seduction which does not necessarily include any physical contact (e.g. suggestive talk, watching a daughter or sister undress, commenting on her body, leering looks) all of which are harmful and can result in a child being controlled.

4. Myth   Incest is usually non-violent. Force is rarely used.
   Fact   Although seduction is often the only technique needed to involve a child because of the vulnerability of children, force is still very often used.

5. Myth   The effects of incest are minimal, especially when the 'sex play' has been 'age appropriate' and 'gently' introduced. If there has been no physical damage, there is no harm done.
   Fact   Incest is an attack, an invasion of physical, emotional and psychic boundaries. We hear repeatedly that incest victims were not harmed. Even the 'mildest' forms of incest can have longlasting effects such as confusion of Self, inability to relate to others or form close friendships, self hatred, internal disorders, personality dissociation (splitting of the personality) or tendency toward addictions. This myth is used to excuse incest.

6. Myth   Incest is not biologically harmful, is not usually painful, and may in some cases be beneficial.

Fact   The effects of incest range from confusion and
       vulnerability to attacks of the same nature, to
       extreme physical disability, including dislocated
       bones, crippling of the joints, ulcers, numbness,
       paralysis and suicidal tendencies. There is noth-
       ing beneficial about incest.

7. Myth   It is not the incest itself that is harmful. What
          is more harmful is the social stigma that the
          child faces when 'the secret' gets out.
   Fact   It is true that due to social mystification and
          public narrow-mindedness a child may get hurt when
          known as an incest victim. However, this statement
          passes off one painful situation onto another. In-
          cest itself is harmful, and social ignorance is
          doubly harmful.

8. Myth   If the child had pleasurable feelings, the incest
          wasn't harmful.
   Fact   A child or teenager may feel sexually excited as
          an automatic, uncontrollable response to being
          sexually manipulated. This is often one of the
          most confusing and damaging aspects of incest, as
          it can lead to extreme confusion and guilt, feel-
          ings of complicity, and a difficulty in later be-
          ing able to separate sexual experiences with
          others from the original attack. Pleasurable feel-
          ings become a horror of feeling a lack of control
          and a sense of body betrayal.

9. Myth   The younger the victim, the less traumatic the
          incest.
   Fact   This comes from the erroneous view that what a
          child does not understand or may not remember,
          won't hurt her. Incest is traumatic at any age.
          To be raped at such an early age (the average age
          of onslaught is four years old), is to have one's
          childhood ripped away. Women are remembering back
          to infancy, and describing feelings of pain and
          humiliation vividly.

10. Myth   The greatest damage is inflicted in adolescence.
    Fact   There is no point to comparing the ages at which a
           victim suffers most. Incest is traumatic and
           damaging at any age.

11. Myth   If a victim defends the attacker or the incest,
            this is proof of her complicity or willingness to
            take part.
    Fact   A victim may defend the incest out of a natural
            tendency to defend her own family or her own
            actions.

12. Myth   Male victims are more hurt than female victims.
    Fact   This myth could be placed with the theory that
            boys are more valuable than girls. It comes from
            the insensitive idea that while a male victim may
            have difficulty achieving an erection, a female
            victim can always open her legs. It comes from a
            general acceptance of rape of females, with the
            attitude that women 'can get over it.' Incest is
            damaging to both female and male victims. Male
            victims often become rapists later, as a retalia-
            tion for the initial hurt and humiliation.

13. Myth   Brother/sister incest is normal, harmless sexual
            curiosity, unless there is a wide (four to five
            years) age span.
    Fact   Brother/sister incest is rampant in Canada, and is
            far from harmless. To say that it is normal and
            harmless is to ignore the number of sisters who
            are forcibly raped by brothers, and often broth-
            ers' friends. Rarely is it consentual, and even
            'consentual incest' among siblings can be a result
            of seduction. Because of the more powerful posi-
            tion held by males in this society, brothers even
            close to the same age as their sisters have been
            able to force sex. The problem lies in what boys
            are learning from men. Sex is pushed as manly, and
            for many young men, sisters are the most access-
            ible, as they try to prove themselves to other
            men, through sexual exploits.

14. Myth   Brother/sister incest happens in crowded, dull
            families.
    Fact   Brother/sister incest happens in all kinds of
            families.

15. Myth   Incest happens in poor, disorganized, unstable
            families.

Fact   Incest is being discovered in poor, disorganized
and unstable families, because these families
often come to the attention of the social services. Incest, however, happens in every type of
family, including rich familites that look 'perfect,' Often families that appear perfect are very
hard to get away from.

16. Myth   Incest is caused by stress, poor family relations
or sexual dysfunction within the marriage.
Fact   None of these reasons need result in incest, and
many women are not 'withholding' sex. Some have
lost interest in sex, for valid reasons. There is
a tendency to excuse men who are raping, to examine their 'needs' and to find ways to 'meet these
needs.' 'Needs' are used as excuses. Wives are examined for why they do not want to be sexual,
while men are rarely questioned about why they
'need' sex to the degree they do, or in the ways
they do. Little emphasis is put on the problem of
what training men receive socially, in relating
sexually (and non-sexually) to adult women.

17. Myth   The parents are immature, unable to set limits.
Fact   This lumps both parents together, blaming mothers for
what fathers or sons are doing. In many families, the
mother is mature, sensitive and caring, and limits
are normal. It has been recognized that many fathers,
however, are found to be controlling and severe.

18. Myth   Confrontation with the law and schools come from a
victim's having poor parental guidance, not from
the incest itself. Incest victims tend to use the
incest to account for these problems.
Fact   These confrontations are often a direct result of
the incest, and this myth draws blame back onto
'the parents' rather than looking at the incest
itself. The danger in this misinterpretation is
that an incest victim can become confused into believing that she is not looking realistically at
other problems, when in fact she has just begun to
understand the root of the original one.

19. Myth   Incest is multi-generational, transmissible from
mother to daughter.

Fact   It is easy to say that incest is multi-generational
       when it has been going on for centuries, and when
       so many of us are discovering that our mothers are
       also incest victims. The emphasis here is wrongly
       placed as a defect in character, transmissible
       from mother to daughter, rather than a defect in
       the character of the men doing the raping. Numbers
       are used against the individuals, rather than
       pointing to a widespread social problem.

20. Myth   Incest is caused by men's reluctance to 'go out-
           side of the family,' to prostitutes, to satisfy
           their 'needs.'
    Fact   Many men who claim that they wanted to avoid com-
           plications by staying 'within the family' are ex-
           cusing themselves for using women who are access-
           ible to them. Many do in fact go to prostitutes,
           and/or have affairs. A major proportion of ser-
           vices offered by prostitutes cater to men who want
           'a young girl.' Whether or not an attacker has
           'gone outside' the family, the attacking of chil-
           dren is a sign of men's belief that 'his' family
           is his property, a concept still condoned by so-
           ciety. This myth is used to draw sympathy to the
           attacker.

21. Myth   Court is more harmful than the incest itself.
    Fact   This is an attempt to avoid what may well be dis-
           astrous court procedures by warning (or threaten-
           ing) us with the idea that it is better not to lay
           charges. Incest has usually been more harmful than
           the court procedures, and there is little hope for
           attackers changing without police intervention.
           The problem of double revictimization will not be
           solved until court attitudes change.

22. Myth   Incarceration is damaging to the attacker.
    Fact   Again, this is a plea not to charge attackers,
           disregarding the safety of the victims. Incarcera-
           tion is damaging inasmuch as Canada is lagging be-
           hind in proper programmes for attackers.

23. Myth   Incarceration usually happens.
    Fact   Most men are rarely charged. The testimony of
           children is rarely accepted. Collaborative evi-

dence (a witness) is required when none is available.

24. Myth   Focussing on prevention of reoccurrence is apt to
cause guilt.
    Fact   Prevention of reoccurrence is the most important
aspect to consider. This is the reason that help
has been sought. The myth about guilt is a protection of the attacker, and this attitude is dangerous to the victim.

25. Myth   Couple therapy will solve many problems, and can
result in the family remaining together.
    Fact   Although some meetings between a wife and an in-
cestuous husband may be helpful at some point in
sorting out what happened, allowing the woman to
confront the attacker, arranging for separation,
etc., this should be at the discretion of the
woman herself. Many women and children complain of
having been forced to meet with an attacker when
they preferred to get away, start a new life,
never see him again. Women are being pressured by
social workers, psychiatrists and others to 'keep
the family together,' and women who have been separated temporarily are not being given a chance or
the proper support to start over again on their
own. Couple therapy is usually focussed on reunit-
ing the parents, and on sexual therapy. A woman,
then, who may have been dissatisfied with the marriage, is pressured to give her husband 'what he
needs,' after hearing that he has raped her daugh-
ter(s) or son(s). This is more equivalent to
torture, than to a solution.

26. Myth   Family meetings are a successful method of resolving problems.
    Fact   Family meetings can be an important part of the
healing process, but not when the attacker is included. Including the attacker, especially at the
beginning before the rest of the family is ready,
places the victim(s) in a dangerous position both
physically and mentally. Victims' stories may be
retracted under the pressure of premature confrontation, and feelings of guilt from disclosure
can cause victims to give more power to the

attacker, rather than less. Including the attacker in family meetings before the other members are strong, can cause the attacker to believe that he can get away with the incest, and gives him a chance to form alliances with defensive family members, who may not want to believe that the incest happened. Above all, family meetings that include the attacker bind the mother and victim(s) to him, preventing any chance to make independent decisions about the route they want to take.

27. Myth   Keeping the family together is the best solution, for economic reasons.

    Fact   This is evidence of just how little the feelings of women and children are taken into account by economists in a money-oriented society. The problems that single mothers face, and the lack of opportunity for women on the labour market need to be solved, rather than sacrificing the mother and the victim(s) to life with a man who has been violent toward them.

28. Myth   It is not so much the attacker's fault, as a family problem caused by the family 'constellation.'

    Fact   This philosophy is used to spread around the blame and the real origin of the problem. There is a reluctance to look directly at the amount of violence by men toward women and children. Blaming the women and children for what a man has thought up and forced, is a way of hiding behind innocent people. The problem lies in what men are teaching men.

29. Myth   Incest is a secret kept within the family, by the structional pattern of the family.

    Fact   This lends to the theory that everyone colludes and has a vested interest in the incest continuing. Usually the attacker and the victim are the only ones who know, and sometimes the victim is threatened with her life to keep quiet. Victims may also block out the memory of a rape without realizing it, in order to survive.

30. Myth   The daughter takes part in the incest out of hatred of her mother.

Fact  Daughters are either forced or seduced into incest, and will sometimes blame their mothers for
not protecting them, believing that their mothers'
power and options are equal to their fathers'.
Certainly there may be a competetive dynamic set
up through the incest between mother and daughter.  The harm done to the mother-daughter relationship is usually underestimated and often mis-
interpreted. Mother-daughter battles are often set
up in clever ways by fathers intent on winning
their daughters' favour.

31.  Myth  Sisters become jealous of the special relationship
between another sister and their father.
Fact  Despite the occasional jealousy over unfair division of attention, and treats that have no explanation, most sisters describe feelings of horror
and protectiveness, not jealousy, toward sisters
who they know are being raped.

32.  Myth  The daughter later clings to her mother out of
guilt for past anger.
Fact  This is a negative way to describe a daugher's attempts later in life to repair her bond with her
mother, and to drop guilt for past emotions con-
nected to the incest.

33.  Myth  Mothers suffer from a lack of ability to give nurturance, or to protect their children, affectional
neglect of children, role reversal with daughters,
frigidity, inability to 'give sex,' loss of personal identity, fear of separation, unconscious
agreement with the incest, insecurity of their
femininity or self worth, overdependence on their
mothers, absorption in their own infantile needs,
denial, promiscuity, sexual indifference, emotional distance, incompetance, depression, intimidation, denial of mother and wife duties, need to be
a child, lack of caring in own childhood, institu-
tionalization or desertion by own parents, inability to learn their role as mother, weak re-
straints against the sex taboo, ambivalence toward
their own mothers, overinvolvement with their own
mothers, cold, rejecting, hard, callous, poor
housekeepers, intellectually dull. They frequently

know and then pretend surprise, set their daughters up in their roles, and set their daughters'
rooms next to their husbands'.

Fact   Mothers may fit one or several of these characteristics. Most women do, as we have been trained in
these directions. These are not the cause of incest. What is appalling is the amount of focus and
analysis of the mothers' personalities, while
fathers and sons go relatively unnoticed, or suffer less harsh criticism. Mothers are victims of
the incest, just as their children are. A woman
may be controlled by her husband's violence, or by
his denials of her suspicions. Most mothers were,
and are, caring mothers. They do not 'set their
daughters up.'

34. Myth   Most mothers know on some level.
    Fact   Most do not know.

35. Myth   Mothers aren't told because they have already
           failed their children.
    Fact   Mothers aren't told for many reasons. The child
           victim may correctly perceive that her mother will
           be too shocked to believe her (at least at first)
           or she may fear hurting her mother by admitting
           that her father or brother (uncle, grandfather,
           etc.) has made sexual advances. She may fear being
           blamed. The child's dilemma and the mother's ter-
           rible and painful position are usually minimized,
           and a mother's difficulty in coping seen as a per-
           sonal defect.

36. Myth   Incest is caused by a mother deserting her chil-
           dren.
    Fact   This does not take into account the vast majority
           of women who do not leave their children, and it
           is an aggressive stab at women who have been
           forced to leave their children, for instance in
           leaving violent marriages, in order to save their
           own lives. It doesn't take into account that in
           court, men who contest custody usually win, and
           that most men who are accused of incest or sexual
           assault get off, for lack of evidence. This myth
           puts the blame for incest on any woman who leaves
           the house for any reason, whether it be shopping,
           or a night out for herself.

37. Myth   Daughters who are incest victims are needy, de-
           prived children.
    Fact   This gives the impression that there is something
           wrong with the daughter or with the attention that
           has been received from the mother. It fits in with
           the theory that the father was combining his
           'needs' with his daughter's. Nothing a child does
           makes her or him responsible for incest.

38. Myth   Daughters who are incest victims are often mature
           for their age, taking their mother's role, being
           responsible for household tasks.
    Fact   Responsibility, maturity and capability are seen
           as a complicated 'come-on' to a confused father.
           This is not a cause of incest, it is being used as
           an excuse.

39. Myth   Incest can satisfy a child's need for physical
           affection.
    Fact   This theory comes from a growing 'pro-incest'
           lobby. It comes from the idea that incest is not
           harmful, and excuses men who claim to have had the
           child's best interests at heart.

40. Myth   The child is seductive, and often responsible for
           the arousal.
    Fact   She is never responsible for the arousal, even
           when she has been taught to act seductively.

41. Myth   If it happened, the child was asking for it.
    Fact   A child never asks for it.

42. Myth   The daughter colludes with her father in most
           cases.
    Fact   Although it may appear that a father and daughter
           team up against a mother, the father is respon-
           sible for the seduction. A daughter never colludes
           without having been seduced into it.

43. Myth   Fathers turn to daughters and sons for warmth and
           nurturance.
    Fact   The majority of men have been nurtured by their
           own mothers, their wives, and other women along
           the way. This is used as an excuse.

44. Myth   Some fathers are submissive.

      Fact   Even fathers who appear submissive are aggressive, in their having initiated the incest.

45. Myth  Some fathers are expressing true and deep love and affection.
      Fact   This myth excuses and condones incest. Incest is not an act of love, it is a violation.

46. Myth  Some incest victims become lesbians to escape solving problems, or because of feeling rejected by their mothers. They go on to choose roles or choose a mother replacement, satisfied with shallow feelings and a limited understanding of a profound relationship.
      Fact   These are but a few of the vicious and damaging myths about lesbians. Many lesbians are incest victims, and many incest victims will decide to be lesbians. (One in ten women are lesbians.) This has nothing to do with escapism, roles or mother replacements. Lesbians are often more, not less healthy than heterosexual women from insisting on a freedom from roles and from a strength built in facing social discrimination.

47. Myth  Talking about incest, staying in the past, serves no purpose.
      Fact   This has been used as a reasoning to dissuade group discussion for women who are incest victims, women who are mothers of incest victims, or men who are incest victims. In fact, those who have found groups have discovered that they are not alone, and have gained considerable strength from discussing common experiences and solutions.

48. Myth  Women-only groups are unhealthy, and are used to avoid men.
      Fact   Incest survivors across the country have stated again and again that without the safety and security found in women-only groups, they would not have spoken about the incest, or not to the extent that they have been able to. Many are certain that they would not even have been able to fully remember the details, with a man present. Despite these statements, men continue to describe themselves as 'experts,' bent on proving that 'not all men are

bad,' to women (including very young women) who
have just been raped. Women-only groups provide a
place for us to speak and learn about our Selves
as women. We need that time.

49. Myth  Some cultures consider incest to be healthy.
    Fact  Many justify incest with this philosophy, and it
          has been used generally to confuse people, and to
          condone incest. No matter what country, no matter
          what culture, incest is harmful and must be
          stopped. A woman in another part of the world is
          just as hurt and robbed of her life as a woman
          here. Religious and cultural freedom do not exist
          for women (or men) who are being raped or seduced
          as children.

50. Myth  Incest victims are scarred for life.
    Fact  Some incest survivors dispute this, and some take
          offence to the way in which this phrase is used.
          As a statement, it promotes the idea that incest
          survivors carry some imperfection for life, and
          that an incest survivor is therefore not capable
          of clear thinking. Given current statistics this
          implicates one third of all women. It encourages
          people to not look at their own lives, to stand
          apart and analyse, and to too often discriminate
          against incest survivors. It is through the
          bravery of incest survivors speaking out that we
          have learned as much as we have and begun to un-
          derstand what needs to be done. Rather than assum-
          ing that all incest survivors are scarred for
          life, what is needed are extensive, free services
          that increase the chances of women living full and
          integrated lives.

Reprinted with the permission of the author. Copies of this
paper can be obtained free of charge from the Healing Centre
for Women, Box 4861, Station E, Ottawa, Ontario, Canada, K1S
5J1. A suggested donation of $2.00 would be appreciated.

Editor's Note: Some of the facts contained in this paper,
may be the author's opinion.

2. THE PREVENTION OF CHILD SEXUAL ABUSE: AN OVERVIEW OF
NEEDS AND PROBLEMS

DAVID FINKELHOR

Child sexual abuse prevention is a new and rapidly growing
field. Although eductional programs about prevention did not
begin to appear until the late 1970s, several years behind
programs designed to identify and treat sexual abuse, dozens
of such programs and a significant number of publications
have appeared across the country during the last two years.

Needs of Children

The appeal of prevention rests on a number of realities
about the problem. First, as several general population
surveys have shown, an important percentage of all children
will likely suffer such abuse. According to a recent random
sample survey of 521 families in the Boston metropolitan
area, 9% of the parents said one of their children had been
a victim of an attempted or completed incident of sexual
abuse. Fifteen per cent of the mothers and 5% of the fathers
said they themselves had been victimized when they were
children (Finkelhor, 1984). Diana Russell (1983) found in a
random sample of 930 adult San Francisco women that 28% had
been sexually abused before the age of 14. It is becoming
increasingly clear that child sexual abuse is a problem of
serious *public health* proportions.
  Secondly, in spite of the recent increase in the avail-
ability of treatment services to victims of child sexual
abuse, it is clear that most child victims of sexual abuse
will not at any time in the near future be identified, let
along provided with help. All evidence clearly indicates
that most children do not reveal their victimizations, and
when they do, families are still unlikely to seek help
(Finkelhor, 1984). Thus treatment programs can only be expected to assist a small percentage of victims. Some other
broader approach is needed.

The logic of prevention also grows out of experience in
working with victims. Such experience suggests that many
children could have been spared abuse if they had had simple
pieces of information, for example, about their right to refuse sexual advances or about the inappropriateness of the
behaviour that an adult engaged in. It makes obvious sense
to try to provide children with such information early in
their lives in order to learn if this can reduce the toll.

Many prevention efforts are targeted directly at children
through a variety of media. Programmess like the Illusion
Theater of Minneapolis (Kent, 1979) and the Child Assault
Prevention (CAP) programme of Columbus (Cooper, Lutter, &
Phelps, 1983) go directly into schools, where the groups'
trained staff conduct workshops for children at all grade
levels (Brassard, Tyler, & Kehle, 1983). Authors of children's literature have written story books and created
colouring books with titles such as *Red Flag, Green Flag*
(Williams, 1980) to teach children how to avoid sexual
abuse. A number of films, including *Who Do You Tell* and *No
More Secrets*, have been produced, primarily for use in the
schools (Dietrich, 1981). In Seattle, advertising campaigns
with famous people such as basketball star Bill Russell have
been used to teach children to identify possible child
molesters.

Prevention efforts have been directed toward a very broad
spectrum of children. This strategy has been reinforced by
two important facts which have emerged from contemporary
research on sexual abuse. First, it is apparent that boys
are subject to victimization as well as girls (Finkelhor,
1984). Thus prevention education is usually conducted in
mixed classrooms, and both boys and girls are used as models
in the media. Secondly, children are victimized at an alarm-
ingly early age. Estimates from some research indicate that
a quarter of all abuse occurs before age seven (Finkelhor,
1984). This highlights the need to bring prevention information to quite young children.

Some prevention educators have also recognized that there
are special populations of children who need special approaches, including those who are handicapped and those who
have already suffered victimization. For example, the
Minnesota Program for Victims of Sexual Assault has developed, specifically for disabled adolescents, a prevention
curriculum which tries to take into account the fact that
parents and the rest of society give such children a less
comprehensive amount of basic sex information than is given
to their able-bodied peers (O'Day, 1983).

In regard to children who have already suffered victimization, many treatment programmes started to offer prevention
education only after they became aware that previously
abused children were at high risk for reabuse and that prevention skills could be an excellent vehicle for restoring
their sense of security and self-esteem (Berliner, 1983);
Snowden, 1983). Hoever, since some victimized children will
be present in almost any audience, all prevention programmes
have to take their special needs into account. Illustrating
these special needs, one leading prevention educator, Linda
Sanford (1983), cautions against formulating concepts (such
as 'never keep a secret') in a way that will make already
victimized children feel worse because they did something
they shouldn't have. She favors dealing with this problem by
presenting children with options rather than with absolutes.

Needs of Parents

As an alternative or supplement to direct approaches to
children, some prevention education has been aimed at parents. This education has taken the form of parent groups or
commercially published books such as Sanford's *The Silent
Children* (1980). Such education has some distinct advan-
tages. If parents learn to educate children themselves,
these children would then be receiving repeated exposures to
information from a trusted source, something that a classroom presentation cannot parallel.

However, it is clear that, at the present time, parents
are a long way from providing such information in an accurate and useful way. Some of the inadequacies of current
parental handling of sexual abuse prevention became apparent
in the aforementioned survey of 521 parents of children ages
six to fourteen in the Boston metropolitan area (Finkelhor,
1984): (1) Only 29% of the parents said they had had a discussion with their child specifically related to the topic
of sexual abuse. (2) Even when such discussion had occurred,
in many cases they failed to include a mention of important
aspects of the problem. Only 53% of discussions, for example, mentioned the possibility of abuse by an adalt ac-
quaintance, only 22% by a family member. Only 65% mentioned
the possibility of someone trying to take off the child's
clothing. (3) Often the discussions that did occur took
place too late. Most parents believed the optimal age for
talking about sexual abuse with a child was around age nine.
Based on the parents' own childhood experiences, however,

statistics indicated that over a third of all those who
suffer sexual abuse are victimized before age nine.

Why do parents have such difficulty teaching their children about child sexual abuse? The survey and the follow-up
discussions with parents suggested some answers. A number of
parents simply did not visualize sexual abuse as a serious
risk to their child. They tended to think of their own child
as well supervised, as able to avoid danger. Sixty-one per
cent thought their neighbourhood was safer than average and
only 4% thought their neighbourhood less safe. Another reason given for not telling children about sexual abuse was
the fear of unnecessarily frightening the child. Parents
said they were afraid both of creating additional anxiety
and of possibly making the child suspicious of all adults.
While these parents are certainly sincere in their concern,
prevention educators point out that parents warn children
about strange animals without worrying that it will make
them afraid of all animals, or about cars without worrying
that they may never want to learn to drive (Sanford, 1980).

It is particularly curious that virtually all parents warn
children about the possibility of kidnapping. The idea that
someone might try to take the child away must certainly be a
far more frightening idea to a child than the idea that
someone might try to fondle his/her genitals, particularly
since children have a very alarming awareness of separation
but a rather vague one of sex. The contrast is particularly
ironic insofar as kidnapping is a far less likely event in a
child's life than sexual abuse. Thus the fact that parents
all warn children about it suggests that the anxiety they
are trying to avoid is not their child's but their own.
Also, kidnapping may be much easier to talk about than
sexual abuse because parents have ready-made formulas for
discussing the subject. Every parent has heard phrases like
'don't get in a car with (or take candy from) a stranger,'
which he/she can repeat. Similar formulas have not existed
in the past concerning sexual abuse, which means that parents, confronted with the need to bring up the subject, have
to improvise, using their own confused knowledge. This prospect has led many of them to avoid the issue. Efforts are
now being made by prevention educators, such as Linda
Sanford and Cordelia Anderson, to provide formulas for parents, and these may make the process easier.

A more profound problem for parents in talking about sex-
aul abuse and a feature of sexual abuse that differentiates
it from kidnapping, is that it concerns sex. Most parents

have a notoriously difficult time talking to their children about sexual topics of all sorts, and this difficulty generalizes to sexual abuse (Roberts, Kline, & Gagnon, 1978). Parents often feel they lack the knowledge, vocabulary, and practice to speak about sexual matters. They are afraid of embarrassing themselves in front of their children by appearing ignorant, tongue-tied, or confused. Secondly, sexual topics trigger strong emotional feelings for parents, reminders of sexual traumas or disappointments in their own lives. Thirdly, parents are unsure of their own values in such matters and are aware that sexual discussions may oblige them to talk about their own feelings and opinions or even personal experiences.

A question of some importance for parent education efforts is whether there are particularly high-risk children whose parents should be specially targeted. One consistent finding about risk is that children who live in stepfamilies are unusually vulnerable (Finkelhor, 1981; Giles-Simes & Finkelhor, 1984; Russell, 1983). This suggests directing some special sexual abuse awareness information to custodial parents who are marrying or remarrying. Another group of parents with some special needs may be those who were themselves victimized when they were children. Many workers in the field are of the opinion that children of such parents are at high risk, although no good research data have yet confirmed this point. Understandably, some of these parents have an extraordinarily difficult time raising these issues with their children because of the painful memories they restimulate.

Also to be considered are parents from different ethnic backgrounds and different social classes who need to be educated in a manner and with concepts consistent with their own specific backgrounds and needs. In a diverse country like the United States, this makes it more difficult to design a single approach that can be effective with everyone. One interesting finding from the Boston study, however, was the uniformity with which parents of all classes and ethnic groups abdicated their responsibility for discussing sexual abuse. Parents who had more education or high occupational status definitely did not do a better job than those who were poorly educated or came from a lower social class. There were also no differences along racial, ethnic, or religious lines. This does suggest that equivalent if not identical problems confront parents in all social groups, and that no group should be assumed to be superior.

Current Concepts in Prevention

Despite some disagreements among the variety of groups offering approaches to sexual abuse prevention, what is for
the most part striking about these approaches is their sim-
ilarity. These educators have had to confront a common set
of challenges, and have resolved them in common fashion. The
nature of the common challenge might be outlined as follows:
  (1) Sexual abuse, as adults generally talk about it, is a
complicated idea, involving concepts of appropriate sexual
behaviour, appropriate sexual partners, ethics, and social
obligations. These concepts are not ones that are readily
grasped by children, especially young children. Prevention
programmes need to translate the notion of sexual abuse into
concepts that make sense within the world of the child.
  (2) The notion of sexual abuse is also one that has large
and frightening overtones for adults and the resulting ten-
sion is easily passed on to children. As CAP educators point
out, children who are simply made to feel frightened and
powerless may be even less capable of avoiding abuse. Prevention programmes have wanted to find some way to avoid or
moderate the potentially fearsome overtones of the issue.
  (3) Sex education is still a controversial matter in many
communities in the U.S. As a result, teachers, and particularly school administrators who in most American communities
are politically vulnerable officials, are very reluctant to
permit anything that appears controversial in regard to sex
to be included in the educational curriculum.
  Prevention programmes have used very creative solutions to
confront these challenges. For example, consider the question of how to make sexual abuse meaningful to younger children. For the most part, educational programmes have tried
to relate the problem of sexual abuse to other kinds of
problems that children do readily grasp (Hutchinson &
Chevalier, 1982; Crisci, 1983). The CAP programmes start
their explanations of sexual abuse by talking about bullies
and illustrating the discussion with a skit of an older
child trying to coerce money from a younger child. Being the
victim of a bully is a kind of experience presumably all
children can relate to. In this context, the explanation of
sexual abuse (illustrated by a role-play where an uncle
tries to coerce a kiss from his little niece) is readily
understood.
  The members of the Illusion Theater group make sexual
abuse comprehensible by putting it in the context of what

# 22 David Finkelhor

they call the Touch Continuum. They start out by discussing
the differences between touching that feels good (also
called 'nurturant' or 'positive' touch, illustrated by hugs,
pats, snuggles, etc.) and touching that feels bad (also
called 'exploitative,' 'manipulated,' or 'forced' touch, illustrated by hitting, bullying, trapping). The group also
has a category of what they call 'confusing' touch ('touch
that mixes you up or makes you feel funny') that includes
touches that convey double messages. In this context they
introduce sexual abuse as a form of touch that feels either
bad or confusing (Kent, 1979). The Touch Continuum has been
much borrowed and adapted, often ending up as a dichotomy
between the good and the bad or, as one adaptation puts it,
'Red Flag vs Green Flag touches' (Williams, 1980). Obviously, talking about good and bad touch involves a vocabulary
very readily understood by even small children.

   The use of metaphors about bullies and touching has another effect: it makes the discussion of sexual abuse seem
less like sex education. Prevention programmes usually talk
about their goals as ones of personal safety or assult prevention or empowerment, not sex education. Although there
are variations from programme to programme and setting to
setting, depending on the sensitiitvies involved, most programmes are designed so that the subject of sex can be
skirted; sexual activities do not have to be explicitly
named; words generally associated with sex or sex education
do not have to be explicitly used. In some programmes, sexual organs are not referred to by their proper names; references are made instead to such things as 'private zones'
(Dayee, 1982), 'molestation,' 'touching in private areas,'
'touching all over,' 'touching under the panties,' and
'places usually covered by a bathing suit.' With some important exceptions, the formal curricula of most programmes
do not try to provide children with other kinds of sex education, such as information about sexual anatomy or vocabulary.

   Another device that has been common to almost all programmes has been to use humour and entertainment, avoiding
presentations that are dry and serious. They usually involve either theatre, role playing, puppets, or colouring
books. They are also very participatory, asking children to
get involved. This entertainment format engenders a light
tone that has allayed adults' anxieties about frightening
the children.

Programmes have also relied on other devices to undercut the potentially frightening element. For one thing, they have not tended to illustrate the more frightening forms of sexual abuse, ones that go on over extended periods of time or that involve great amounts of violence. A variety of programmes include such illustrations as an older brother who always comes into the bathroom when his little sister is showering, an uncle who wants a highly sexual kiss, or a man who wants to put his hands into a child's panties (Hutchinson & Chevalier, 1982; Williams, 1980).

The programmes have also tried to temper the potentially fear-generating aspects by emphasizing positive actions children can take to handle such situations. They encourage children to believe that they have 'rights': the right to control their own body, the right to be 'safe, strong, and free' (Cooper et al. 1983), the right not to have someone touch them in a way that feels bad, the right to keep their body private. Armed with these notions about rights, children learn how to say 'no' to abusers. In more comprehensive programmes, they are also taught how to be assertive of their rights and their safety, even in the face of adults who insist otherwise. In the CAP programme, they act out situations to help one another find ways to say 'no.' They brainstorm strategies for getting away from or out of dangerous situations. Some programmes teach certain self-defense techniques, such as yelling and getting assistance from a friend. The CAP programme has a special yell which is practiced by participants in all their classes.

All programmes place a very strong emphasis on the idea that children must tell someone right away, reflecting the reality that most children in the past have not. To encourage them to share their experience, programme leaders carefully explain to the children the ways in which offenders will usually try to intimidate them so that they will keep the experience secret, and why such intimidation should be ignored. One of the concepts that has gained great popularity in prevention education involves making the distinction between a secret and a surprise (Sanford, 1980). Secrets, which you are *never* supposed to tell, are a bad idea, but surprises, which you will tell someone about later in order to make them happy, are okay. Sometimes children are also alerted to the fact that not all adults will necessarily believe them and they are urged to persist until they find someone who does. These avoidance, resistance, and help-

seeking techniques are intended to help children avoid victimization and instill in them the feeling of being em-
powered rather than frightened.

## Organizational Issues

Most prevention programmes have devoted serious attention to
the approach to the community in which they will be presented. Although this is not always an aspect which can easily be communicated or transferred to other communities as a
package, it is a crucial part of the current prevention efforts. As mentioned earlier in the discussion of concepts,
one can find, within a variety of organizational frameworks,
a consensus about certain common elements considered indis-
pensable to prevention. To begin with, it is clear that the
successful prevention programmes define what they are doing,
not merely in terms of how it is related to the community.
They have thought through political and organizational issues, and although their ultimate goal may be the education
of children, much of their initial effort is directed to the
community as a whole. Successful prevention programmes generally do a great deal of work to create the proper climate
for gaining entry into a community. This includes developing
a cadre of influential people who support the use of the
programme and who can lobby on its behalf. Of course, the
extension of long-established programmes is made easier by
the solid reputation acquired on the basis of their prior
work.
  Once school systems become interested, one of the first
steps most organizers of school-oriented prevention programmes take is to present the material to parents and professionals in advance of any presentation to the children
themselves. This is an effective way of diffusing any opposition and allaying anxieties about the programme and also
of educating other important audiences. Prevention programmes usually recruit some local individuals to receive
intensive training. This serves a number of functions. These
individuals, often teachers or other school personnel, can
assist the leaders in presenting the school programme, and
because they are more likely to know the children, can thus
project additional credibility. They are also instrumental
in helping the programme have a sustained effect since, as
individuals within the system, they will continue to convey
prevention concepts long after the trainers have left.

Another practice of responsible prevention programmes is
to prepare the community for the influx of reports of sexual
abuse which are inevitably generated by the education and
training. Any professionals, including classroom teachers or
school guidance counselors, who are going to be involved in
the prevention programme or its follow-up, need to be trained in how to deal with reports from children. Some of the
programmes, eg, CAP, make their own staff available to receive such reports by scheduling time after the presentation
when children who have special questions can come and talk
privately. In some communities referral resources are developed by contacting professionals and agencies and then assessing which ones do or do not have the skills to receive
sexual abuse reports.

There appears to be some difference of opinion in the
field over the advisability of getting prevention education
incorporated directly into school curricula. In Seattle,
trainers for the Committee for Children train regular classroom teachers who in turn present the material to the children. The trainers themselves only rarely appear in front of
the classes. Donna James of the Committee feels that this
method is efficient, because trainers do not need to go back
to a school each year, and effective, because students can
get on-going instruction from a person they already know and
trust - their teacher. Other educators, such as Rich Snowden
of San Francisco, prefer a model where outside teachers come
into the school and work with the children. This model in-
sures that the trainers will be true specialists in the
field. Snowden also worries that schools will not give
sufficient support and encouragement to their own staff
specialists in sexual abuse prevention and that these programmes will suffer in times of budget cutbacks.

Conceptual Dilemmas

Solutions to problems can sometimes create new problems.
While the concepts developed by prevention programmes demonstrate a great deal of creativity, they also generate dilemmas. Perhaps the most troublesome dilemma from our point of
view concerns the relationship between sex education and
sexual abuse prevention. As mentioned earlier, in order to
deal with public squeamishness about sex education in
schools, prevention programmes have devised various ways for
skirting direct sexual references and discussions. While

there are programmes that can and do allow for more sexual
content (two that seem to make a particular effort are
'Childproof for Sexual Abuse,' 1981, from Washington State;
and 'Sexuality and Sexual Assault: A Disabled Perspective,'
1983, from Minnesota), this material is not 'required.' The
tendency to avoid it may be particualrly great when less experienced trainers selectively borrow concepts from other
programmes, or when the education is offered in a setting
where sexual subjects could be particularly controversial.

There are a number of possible negative consequences of
sex abuse prevention which avoids explicit sexual content.
For one thing, there is some question about whether, under
such conditions, children truly learn what sexual abuse is.
The problem is especially acute in some of the less graphic
media where stick figures are used or where abuse is described as 'touching all over' or the 'uh-oh feeling.' (Uh-
oh feelings are used in the Renton, Washington, Sexual Abuse
Prevention Program, 1981.) Secondly, children may not be
getting enough practice in using words and phrases to talk
about sexual activity. For a long time there has been a
general consensus among professionals in the field (emphasized quite clearly in Sanford's book, *The Silent
Children*) that children are inhibited from telling about
abuse when they do not have a vocabulary for or experience
in discussing sex-related matters.

Thirdly, the avoidance of explicit sexual content may be
conspicuous and confusing to children. They hear adults saying 'Tell us about it,' while at the same time these adults
are themselves using vague euphemisms and circumlocutions to
talk about sex. For some children, the message behind the
message may be that, in spite of what adults say, they
really do not want to talk about sex in plain terms. Finally, it is worth being concerned about other inferences
children may draw when sexual abuse is talked about in isolation from other aspects of human sexuality. It is possible
that when adults only talk to them about avoiding the coercive forms of sexuality, the children are left with the im-
pression that sex is primarily negative. (For example, one
wonders what underlying message is conveyed by one programme's heroes whose names are 'Hands Off Bill and the
Untouchables,' Martin & Haddad, 1982). It would not be too
hard for children to misinterpret the message and come to feel
guilty about their childhood sex play. Programmes often try
to leaven their approach by talking about positive touch,
affection, or assertive behaviour, but almost never do they
discuss what might be positive and age-appropriate sexuality.

To their credit professionals in the field of sexual abuse prevention are aware of these dilemmas. We have not encountered one who was not in favour of making general sex education available in more of our school systems. The Illusion Theater has even implemented this awareness with a new play, *No Easy Answers*, aimed at the junior and senior high school audiences, which explores the full range of adolescent sexual concerns. Some educators see sex abuse prevention as the vehicle through which sex education will ultimately be accepted by school systems. However, most sex abuse prevention educators are also very realistic. They acknowledge that, if sexual abuse prevention were to be too closely linked to a sex education focus, fewer schools would adopt it and fewer children, especially young children, would be exposed. While most feel that prevention education could be improved with more sex education, they agree that, under present circumstances, the children they reach are at least being given valuable knowledge.

None the less, the relationship between sexual abuse prevention and sex education is an important one that needs further exploration, especially when evaluation research is done (Wall, 1983). Many of us are inclined to believe that lack of sex education is an important component of the sexual abuse problem. Children cannot get adequate information about sexual abuse in a climate where adults in contact with the child feel constrained from ever talking about sex. People working in the sex abuse prevention field need to confront this reality and, whenever and wherever possible, bring pressure and influence and opinion to bear on behalf of more and better sex education for every age group. How can today's and tomorrow's children be well protected from sexual abuse in a setting where adults are fearful of talking with them about sex?

References

Adams, C. & Fay J. *No more Secrets*. San Luis Obispo, Calif.: Impact Publishers, 1981

Berliner, L. *Personal communication*, 1983

Brassard, M.R. Tyler, A.H. & Kehlt, T.J. School programs to prevent intrafamilial child sexual abuse. *Child Abuse and Neglect*, 1983, 31, 241-245

Cooper, S., Lutter, Y., & Phelps, C. *Strategies for free childhood*. Columbus, Ohio: Child Assault Prevention Project, 1983

Crisci, G. *Personal safety curriculum for the prevention of child sexual abuse*. Hadley, Mass., 1983

Dayee, F.S. *Private zone*. Edmonds, Wash.: Charles Franklin Press, 1982

Dietrich, G. Audiovisual materials with critique. In P.B. Mrazek & C.H. Kempe (Eds) *Sexually abused children and their families*. New York: Pergamon Press, 1981

Finkelhor, D. *Sexually victimized children*. New York: Free Press, 1979

Finkelhor, D. Risk factors in the sexual victimization of children. *Child Abuse and Neglect*, 1980, 4, 265–273

Finkelhor, D. *Child sexual abuse: Theory and research*. New York: Free Press, 1984

Giles-Sims, J., & Finkelhor, D. Child abuse in stepfamilies. *Family Relations* (forthcoming)

Hutchinson, B., & Chevalier, E. *My personal safety book*. Fridley, Minn.: Fridley Police Department, 1982

Kent, C. *A Child sexual abuse project: An educational program for children*. Minneapolis, Minn.: Hennepin County Attorney's Office Sexual Assault Services, 1979

Martin, L., & Haddad, J. *What if I say no?* Bakersfield, Calif.: M.H. Cap, 1981

O'Day, B. *Preventing sexual abuse of persons with disabilities*. St. Paul, Minn.: Minnesota Program for Victims of Sexual Assault, Minnesota Department of Corrections

Renton School District, No 402. *Sexual abuse prevention: A unit in safety*. Renton, Wash.: Department of Curriculum Instruction, 1981

Robert, E., Kline, D., & Gagnon, J. *Family life and sexual learning*. Cambridge, Mass.: Project on Human Sexual Development, 1978

Russell, D.E.H. The incidence and prevalence of intra-familial and extrafamilial sexual abuse of children. *Child Abuse and Neglect*, 1983, 7, 133–146

Sanford, L. *The silent children: A parent's guide to the prevention of child sexual abuse*. New York: Anchor Press/Doubleday, 1980

Sanford, L. *Personal communication*, 1983

Snowden, R. Boys and child sexual assault prevention project. Unpublished paper, CAP Training Center of Northern California, San Francisco, Calif., 1983

Stuart, V., & Stuart, C.K. *Sexuality and sexual assault: Disabled perspective*. Marshall, Minn.: Southwest State University, 1983

Wall, H. *Child assault/abuse prevention project: Pilot
    program evaluation.* Concord, Calif.: Mt Diablo Unified
    School, 1983
Williams, J. *Red flag, green flag people.* Fargo, N.D.:
    Rape and Abuse Crisis Center of Fargo-Moorhead, 1980

[Author's Note: Research for this review, and for the table
by Sharon Araji from which the bibliography was compiled,
was funded by the National Centre for Prevention and Control
of Rape. We wish to thank Mary Lystad for her support in
this project, and Ruth Miller and Kathy Hersh for their help
in preparing the manuscript. Cordelia Anderson, Linda
Sanford, and Rich Snowden gave us valuable insights in the
course of research and writing. Members of the Family
Violence Research seminar made helpful comments on an early
draft of the report. The full report from which this article
was derived is one of a series of papers on the subject of
sexual abuse that are available from the Family Violence
Research Program at the University of New Hampshire.]

## 3. MENTAL HEALTH AND THE IN-FAMILY SEXUAL ABUSE OF CHILDREN AND ADOLESCENTS

CHRIS BAGLEY

Abstract

The author addresses basic issues in the sexual abuse of children within the family. Sexual abuse is distinguished from incest. The cultural roots of sexual abuse are discussed, and insights of the feminist model are applied. Various limited studies of incidence and prevalence are reviewed with a view to estimating possible rates of abuse in Canada. Studies linking early sexual abuse with a range of serious physical and psychosocial sequelae are reviewed. The author discusses treatment models and the goals of treatment, and argues strongly for a fundamental value change in society that will eliminate the sexual victimization of children.

## Basic Issues in Child Sexual Abuse

### Definitions

Although the use of the term 'incest' persists to describe sexual assaults on children within the family, incest and child sexual abuse are not synonymous. Incest is a concept which should be defined in anthropological or socio-biological terms, and concerns the aversion towards and the rules and taboos concerning continued sexual relations between closely related people that are likely to result in pregnancy and an alternative family.[3] Incest always concerns sexually mature individuals, usually in a consensual union. The large majority of cases of child sexual abuse do not fulfill these conditions, but involve the sexual coercion and domination of young children of either sex by adults.[4] Sexual abuse of children is usually the act of someone known to the victim, most probably a family member.[5] However,

stepfathers or cohabiters are more likely than biological
fathers to assault children in the home. Legally, incest
involves having sexual intercourse with a close relative;
however, many sexual assaults on children, whether by
relatives or by non-relatives, stop short of actual intercourse. This does not usually make the psychological trauma
of the assault any less serious.[6]

Cultural Issues and Values
Another problem concerns the incest taboo itself: since sexual assaults on children are widespread, either the taboo is
being frequently violated, or else the idea of incest ap-
plies to a different category of adult relationships. The
latter is a much more plausible hypothesis. Florence Rush,
in her historical review of the 'best kept secret,'[7] produces a mass of evidence to show that the sexual exploitation of children has been an integral but undiscussed aspect
of western culture for many centuries. The sexual concern of
males with deflowering the purity and innocence of childhood
led to the obsession of many Victorian males with the exploitation of children, a passion which has borne fruit in
the modern obsession with nymphets and child pornography.
So-called sexual emancipation, Rush argues, had led to the
male fantasy of a utopia in which 'men will never be bur-
dened by emotional traumas, venereal disease, pregnancy,
commitments, responsibilities, charges of rape, statutory
rape or child molestation as the consequence of their sexual behaviour.'

   Sexual abuse of children takes many forms, and is certainly not confined to the intercourse defined by the incest
statute. Sexual abuse can range from the sexualization of
children for commercial purposes (in advertisements or mass
media); to the exploitation of children through pornography;
to various kinds of sexual assault ranging from exposure and
manual interference to the grossest forms of sexual assault
on prepubertal children. The feminist view, which I accept,
is that this sexual exploitation of children, and especially
that within the family context, is made possible by a deep-
rooted value climate which allows males to regard females,
and especially powerless females, as suitable objects for
all kinds of exploitation.

   Adults who sexually assault children, including their own,
are frequently described in the literature as inadequate
personalities who have created or are experiencing disordered
marital relationships, and who often use alcohol.[10] These

clinical profiles don't contradict the argument that child
sexual assault is caused, fundamentally, by a value principal which underpins the exploitation of all children. The
argument asserts that weak and relatively powerless males
use children (usually, but not always, female children) not
only for sexual gratification, but for the exercise of power
and status as well.[11]

## Incidence and Prevalence

The evidence we have suggests that the true incidence of
child sexual assault within a family context is unknown, but
that the phenomenon has almost certainly involved a significant minority of all children, perhaps as many as ten per
cent. Sarafino estimated in 1979 that a total of 336,200
sexual offences of all kinds were committed against children
in the United States each year.[13] This figure, based on
agency reports, is almost certainly an underestimate; other
figures put the figure at between 5 and 15 per cent of the
child population.[14]

   Finkelhor[15] surveyed a population of college students in
the United States, and found that 19 per cent of the women
and 9 per cent of the males had been sexually assaulted by
the age of 16. Girls from lower-income families were more
likely to have been assaulted, as were girls from socially
isolated backgrounds and those from family situations in
which the natural mother was absent. Eleven per cent of the
women in this survey had been assaulted when under age 12 by
someone aged 18 and over, usually someone within their intimate social network. Finkelhor concluded that 'these
figures confirm the growing suspicion that sexual victimization of children is very widespread. They also show that it
is very much a family problem. If we were to extrapolate on
the basis of this data, something we are not really entitled
to do, given the limitations of the sample, we would estimate that about 9 per cent of all women are sexually victimized by a relative, and about one and a half per cent are
involved in father-daughter sex.'

   One of the limitations of these estimates, which Finkelhor
acknowledges, is that children from low-income families
(considered a high-risk group) are less likely to become
college students. In addition, a frequent result of child
sexual assault in the family is disorganized behaviour including dropping out of school, which also makes college
attendance less likely. These two factors would tend to lower
the rate of reported sexual abuse in the college student

the rate of reported sexual abuse in the college student
sample studied; this suggests that Finkelhor's estimates for
the general population may in fact be underestimates.

Another type of study - a non-random survey of a large female population in North America - provided a different perspective.[18] In 1980, 106,000 female readers of the large-
circulation magazine *Cosmopolitan* returned a postal questionnaire to the magazine. Of the self-selected respondents,
11 per cent had experienced sexual relations with a relative
when a child: 5 per cent reported brother-sister relations,
3 per cent father-daughter, and a further 6 per cent reported sexual assault by an uncle, grandparent or other relative. Rape, threats and coercion were frequently featured in
these reports, and only sex between siblings close in age
was subjectively reported to have no harmful psychological
sequelae for the girl. Often the trauma reported was severe
and long-lasting. This interesting survey cannot give accurate estimates for the population at large, but it does give
confirmation of the widespread nature of the problem as well
as the trauma which the assault frequently entails for the
female victim.

Two estimates of the prevalence of the sexual abuse of
children are available from random samples of U.S. adult
populations. Finkelhor surveyed 521 adult men and women in
the Boston area: 12 per cent (15 per cent of the women and 6
per cent of the men) had suffered sexual abuse as children
or adolescents, both within and outside the family.[19] Using
somewhat different definitions, Russell surveyed 930 adult
women in San Francisco.[20] Sixteen per cent of her respondents reported at least one sexual assault within the family
before the age of 18; 12 per cent reported at least one such
experience before they were 14. Only 2 per cent of these
within-family sexual assaults on children were reported to
the authorities. Fathers (including stepfathers) and uncles
were the most likely to commit serious assaults on children
(including forced intercourse). Russell reports a prevalence
of father-daughter sex relations which is five times
Finkelhor's estimate. Generalized to the total U.S. adult
population, Russell's figures would suggest that at least 3
million American women may be suffering from long-term effects of earlier sexual abuse by fathers, stepfathers or
other male relatives.

A number of unpublished Canadian studies, including surveys of high school populations were available to the
Badgley Committee on Sexual Offences Against Children and

sarily agree with the Badgley Commission estimate), is that
at least 5 per cent of all females will, by their sixteenth
birthday, have experienced traumatic sexual assault within a
family context. I estimate, based on this 5 per cent incidence figure (which I consider conservative) and on the
available data on the average length of time over which assaults continue, that the average proportion of children in
elementary and junior high school currently being assaulted
(within the past week) is 0.75 per cent or about 7 or 8 per
1,000. Every elementary school in Canada will, on the most
conservative estimate, have 2 or 3 students who are currently being sexually assaulted within their families. In addition, about five times this number (an increasing number as
the average age of the student increases) will still be suffering trauma as a result of past sexual abuse. None of the
individuals in this estimate will have received any assistance from formal helping agencies for the sexual abuse or
its long-term effects.

The legacy of this trauma stays with an individual for a
lifetime, and the extrapolation of this 5 per cent estimate
to the female population of Canada produces the staggering
estimate that over half a million women are probably suffering impaired mental health associated with the long-term
psychological legacies of childhood sexual assault. Given
the apparent scale of the phenomenon, there is certainly
some logic in the feminist complaint that the sexual assault
of female children is an important aspect of the socialization of women for passivity and personality problems associated with or leading to subordination.[22]

The most frequent evidence on the amount and the harmfulness of child sexual abuse comes from the surveys of patient, client and agency populations. The motivation of a
number of workers (Meiselmann, Renvoize, Forward and
others)[4] - to research the subject has been the realization
that a large number of their female patients in unselected
clinical populations had experienced sexual assault as children, and that those assaults were often causally related to
later clinical problems. Other surveys of runaway teenagers,[24] young drug users,[25] and young prostitutes[26] have
indicated that at least half of these female populations
have been victims of child sexual assault. There is clear
evidence too from systematic clinical studies that these
assaults have an important causal relationship with later
disturbed behaviour.[27]

The Reporting of Sexual Abuse
An important issue is whether the actual incidence of child
sexual assault is increasing, or whether both cultural
values and professional practice are changing in ways which
make it easier for victims to report abuse. It is clear that
1978 was a key year for professional understanding of the
problem of child sexual abuse, with a 'knowledge explosion'
of books and monographs bringing an enlightened focus to
understanding the problems, its consequences and its treatment.[29] Previously, reports on the topic had been sparse,
and were often biased in suggesting that the incidence of
sexual assault on children was low; that such assaults were
the result of family dysfunctions in which mothers held a
large share of blame; that often the victims of such assault
were not harmed or traumatized; and that often the child
victims themselves played a seductive role, leading on the
weak but sexually frustrated male. It is astonishing, in
retrospect, that the professional community should have accepted such myths and distortions so passively, and this
should remind us that current practice and concepts in other
areas of child welfare may be similarly biased. On this
model then, the great increase in agency reports of child
sexual abuse[30] is an indication that victims are now more
likely to perceive that such assaults are wrong, that com-
plaining to people outside the family is legitimate, and
that such complaints will bring meaningful help.

   This may be an over-optimistic view, however. The supreme
authority of the family over children is still widely
stressed, and in the private domain of family socialization,
children may have no alternative but to believe the adult
male who tells the child that conformity to sexual domination is necessary along with the other conformities required
of children.

   The coerced silence of the child victim is frequently described in case materials.[12] This silence is one of the many
factors which devastate the self-esteem of the victim, and
make later revelation so difficult. Until recently, a child
who did manage to reveal the assault to outsiders was not
believed; this is probably still the case in many traditional
communities. If the child was believed, she or he was stig-
matized and the offence itself ignored. For help-seeking to
occur, the child has to be assured that the threats against
disclosure are unrealistic or empty, and that professionals

such as teachers, ministers, police, crisis workers, and
social workers will be both sympathetic and effective in
bringing help. All of these ideal conditions are frequently
not met.[31]

Although it is easier now for women and children to escape
from physically and sexually abusive males, alternative sociological forces also make it likely that the amount of
sexual abuse of children within families could be increasing.[32] First of all, the eroticization of childhood by
adults in the 1970s, largely for commercial purposes, may
have accentuated a focus on children as suitable victims for
sexual assault. Family changes may be important too. David
Finkelhor points out that the presence of an unrelated adult
male in a household is a special risk factor for children in
terms of sexual assault: such 'blended' families are increasing as divorce and remarriage rates increase. Another
potent factor is the development in the 1960s and 1970s of
an ideology emphasizing the right of individuals sexual fulfilment. Whether or not rates are rising, the fundamental
problem, Finkelhor argues, remains one of masculine sexuality and the power and dominance which men still exercise in
sexual relationships. The development of the sexual 'free-
doms' of the 1960s and 1970s has, as Florence Rush[7] points
out, operated to the advantage of males rather than females,
and has led to the development of an ideology asserting that
all kinds of sexual fulfilment, including sex with children,
are legitimate kinds of male fulfilment. If sexual abuse of
children is ultimately to diminish, profound value changes
must take place in the whole area of relationships between
men and women.

## The Short-term and Long-term Effects of Child Sexual Abuse

There is no good epidemiological evidence on the short- and
long-term physical, psychological and behavioural sequelae
of earlier child sexual abuse in adolescents and young
adults. The estimates from non-random adult populations suggest, however, that at least a minority of victims carry
profound problems into adulthood. Studies of clinical populations suggest that sexual abuse has many profoundly adverse consequences. Especially in the immediate aftermath of
the assault, children suffer a wide range of psychological
and physical traumas. These short- and long-term sequelae
have profound implications for the whole of the child care
and child welfare system, and make child sexual abuse an

overwhelmingly serious problem. For at least a minority of
the victims, profound and permanent personality damage results which can only be reversed by skilled, intensive and
prolonged individual and group therapy. Unless treated adequately, this personality damage has lifelong consequences.[34]

Hill,[35] in a review of literature on sequelae up to 1980,
lists the following immediate traumas to child victims:

- physical traumas, including vaginal and anal lacera-
  tions;
- infections and venereal disease;
- associated physical abuse including bruises and burns;
- pregnancy and menstrual disorders;
- sleeping and eating problems, bedwetting, thumb-sucking,
  night terrors;
- depression, loss of self-esteem and withdrawal from
  peers;
- learning disabilities or developmental delays;
- running away, drug and alcohol use, subsequent juvenile
  prostitution;
- a pervasive sense of anxiety, fear and terror;
- confusion and guilt surrounding secrecy;
- anger and aggression at siblings and the non-violating
  parent.

The harmful sequelae of child sexual abuse and its links
to other kinds of behavioural problems are illustrated by a
recent study by Silbert,[28] which is quite typical both in
terms of methodology and its findings. Silbert surveyed 200
street prostitutes in San Francisco. Seventy per cent of the
women she located were under 21, and 96 per cent were runaways when they began prostituting, usually as juveniles.
The results, Silbert reports,

> ...are alarming, and contradict commonly held viewpoints
> on prostitution from many aspects. The excessive victim-
> ization, physical and sexual abuse, and learned helpless-
> ness, coupled with the young ages and disturbed back-
> grounds of the women, produce a distressing portrait of
> women trapped in a lifestyle they do not want, and yet
> feel unable to leave. Sixty per cent of the subjects were
> the victims of juvenile sexual exploitation, and most sub-
> jects started running away from home as a result of
> sexual, physical or emotional abuse. Once in the streets,
> they were victimized by both customers and pimps; they
> were beaten, raped, robbed and abused...

The majority of the girls came from middle-class families with a formal religious atmosphere. This was no protection against sexual exploitation of the child by fathers or step-fathers. Seventy per cent of the abused girls suffered repeated sexual assault by the same family member, often for a period of years. Almost all of these child victims lost their virginity as a result of the abuse; but they were trapped in their male-dominated households, and could only escape by running away. Once in the streets the obvious means of survival was through prostitution. The majority of respondents who had been sexually assaulted within their families felt that their drift into prostitution was directly related to the earlier sexual assault.

Our own review of the monograph and journal literature on child sexual abuse in the period 1978 to 1982[29,36] has identified the following sequelae of earlier sexual abuse in adolescents and adults:

- suicidal gestures and attempts (probably in about 5 per cent of all sexually abused girls);
- long-term personality problems, including guilt, anxiety, fears, depression and permanent impairment of self-image (probably in a majority of female victims);
- more acute personality sequelae, including chronic psychosis, self-mutilation, induced obesity, anorexia, hysterical seizures, and a chronically self-punitive lifestyle, a reaction to acute feelings of guilt and self-disgust (probably in about 5 per cent of sexually abused girls);
- running away from home, or removal by judicial and child welfare authorities unaware of or indifferent to the sexual abuse (probably in about 20 per cent of female victims);
- prostitution or sexually dominated or exploited life-style (probably in about 5 per cent of female victims);
- withdrawal, coldness, frigidity or lack of trust in psycho-sexual relationships (probably in about 5 to 10 per cent of female victims);
- aggression, aggressive personality disorder, and chronic delinquency (in about 5 per cent of victims);
- drug and alcohol abuse leading to chronic addiction and health impairment (in about 5 per cent of victims).

Many of these adverse sequelae are linked or overlapping, but I estimate, both from research reports and clinical practice, that at least 25 per cent of girls who are sexually abused within their families have serious long-term problems

abused within their families have serious long-term problems
of adjustment and behaviour, while a further 25 per cent
have at least some chronic personality problems. The
first, most seriously disturbed group features prominently
in caseloads of disturbed, drifting, runaway adolescents;
however, this fact is not well understood by workers in this
field, who continue to treat only the symptoms of the abuse
syndrome, often in a superficial or indeed punitive way.

Finkelhor[37] argues that sexual relations between adults
and children are wrong because children cannot give informed consent, and that arguments against such sexual relationships on empirical grounds have the inherent weakness that
if no harmful outcome can be identified, then the relationships are *ipso facto*, permissible. There are difficulties
with Finkelhor's approach, however. There is a considerable
and persuasive literature on children's rights which main-
tains that children do have a legal and moral right to give
informed consent at an early age in relation to, say medical
and surgical intervention, and by the same token, the right
to refuse interventions and acts which they regard as un-
pleasant or demeaning.[38] Given the possibility of informed
choice, the vast majority of children will, I believe, refuse the sexual advances of adults. The ultimate argument
against the sexual exploitation of children by adults is
that in at least half of the cases, and perhaps in more than
half, long-term and perhaps permanent impairment of mental
health will result. There is no way of telling with any cer-
tainty in advance, which type of child will be most damaged:
the age of the child, the type of assault, and the length of
time over which the assaults take place do not seem to be
good predictors of adult psychosocial outcome. However, the
degree of force and coercion used, with threats to ensure
silence and continued compliance, does appear to be particularly related to long-term harm, especially when the abuser
is a previously trusted authority figure such as a father.[15]

Sexual assault within a family context violates a child's
safety needs, which in Maslow's important developmental
model[40] are fundamental needs for a child. The violation of
these safety needs in the family, the context of total
safety for most children, imposes on the child a situation
of lonely terror in which she is forced to deceive her
mother and engage in sexual practices which she may find
stimulating but simultaneously disgusting. The long-term
effect of this self-disgust is a continued self-hatred and
self-devaluation, and an acute difficulty in many aspects of

will of course vary according to the pre-existing personality, temperament and vulnerability of the child; all too
often, however, the victimized child is one who has poor
self-esteem to begin with, and accepts the abuse as just one
more demeaning burden which adults impose on children. According to Linda Sanford,[41] such a child tells herself:

> I don't like this, but what do I know? I'm never right
> about anything ... I know if I tell anyone about this,
> they'll get mad at me for making trouble ... Nobody else
> likes me, not in the whole world, except for this person,
> so I'll do what he says.

Children with poor ego strength and impaired self-concept
are probably most likely to be victims and are easy to coerce into silence. Children in psychologically open families
are likely to have both a close relationship with their
mother and the ego-strength to resist seductive approaches
from an adult male, as well as the ability to reveal such
abuse immediately.[42]

Treatment Models

The sexual abuse of children often causes profound and long-
lasting damage, so clearly treatment has to be intensive and
prolonged if profound traumas are to be reversed. Two major
treatment programmes led by Suzanne Sgroi[43] and Hank
Giarretto[44] have recently published clinical handbooks giving detailed accounts for innovative practitioners. The
reader is advised to consult these handbooks, as a detailed
account of intensive treatment models cannot be given here.
   Practitioners in this field need to be mature, skilled,
well-educated people, who have come to terms with their own
sexuality and their feelings towards the sexual exploitation
of children. Former victims of abuse who have been through
extensive healing programmes are particularly valuable as
resource people in running self-help groups since they, of
all people, can understand the meaning of abuse and empath-
ize with victims. In Giarretto's programme, victims ('Sons
and Daughters United') and parents, including offenders
('Parents United'), form an important part of an integrated
treatment model.[45] The overall approach to treatment has a
number of fundamental tasks:
   1. To understand and try to change the values of the community, of individuals, and of professionals concerning the
sexual abuse of children.

2. To work towards an integrated response to the concerns of interested parties – the sexually abused child, child protection workers, sex crimes investigators. Crown prosecutors, and specialized therapists, once abuse has been revealed. The result should be a plan of action that serves the fundamental welfare interest of the child or adolescent victim.

3. To engage in a prolonged and intensive treatment programme involving victim, siblings, mother and father with associated self-help groups.

4. To undertake the treatment of adult former victims still suffering long-term effects of earlier sexual abuse.

5. To undertake preventive education with young children to enable them to understand the sexually abusive approaches of others; to give them a healthy self-concept which will enable them to resist these approaches; and to assure them that responsible adults will listen and take appropriate protective action when they complain of abuse.

The need for community education in order to achieve value changes is clear when we understand the traditional reaction to sexual abuse of a child. Even if the child is able to construct a cognitive and moral framework which allows her to understand that the abusive adult behaviour is wrong and can be resisted, she then has to complain to a parent, teacher, minister, relative or counsellor. This person must first of all believe her; many abused children were put down in the past, dubbed as liars. Then the adult has to listen sympathetically, and finally take effective action which will end the abuse in a way which does not further damage the child's self-esteem. These expectations were in the past unlikely to be fulfilled: even when she was believed, a girl was unlikely to obtain effective help. Usually the abuse could only be stopped when she was removed from the house to a children's shelter. Here, in a setting identified with juvenile delinquents and runaways, the victims' concept of herself as a bad or wicked person was likely to be further reinforced.

Value change is crucial if child victims are to receive active, integrated, effective help. In this changed model it is the offender who should be removed from the home, not the victim. Sometimes the teenage girl herself will ask to spend a period with a relative or in a foster home; this wish should be respected. All action taken at the point of disclosure should involve the fullest integration of different services (eg, child welfare workers, special therapy teams, police, and prosecutors). In most jurisdictions, reporting

of child abuse to the director of child welfare is, in
theory at least, mandatory, and at that point police should
also be informed. However, in all of the actions taken by
workers of various kinds there should be one underlying
principle or goal: all actions should serve the best interests of a damaged, unhappy, traumatized young person, and
the goal of all actions should be to enable the girl to re-
cover her sense of dignity, self-respect and self-esteem.[44]

Failure to Meet the Victim's Needs

In most Canadian cities, there is not yet any adequate co-
ordination of services for sexually abused children. Child
welfare or child protection workers unprepared and untrained
for such work can still act with panic, embarrassment or
even denial, remove the child from the home, and leave
things at that. The child is 'punished,' but receives no
therapy related to the sexual abuse at all. Judith Herman
reports the case of a girl moved from home after reporting
sexual assault:

> The director of the institution where I was placed had
> been trained as a counsellor. What I resent about her now
> is that I lived there for four years, and even though she
> knew what had happened, she never once took me aside and
> said, 'Would you like to talk about it?' From age fourteen
> to eighteen I had nobody to help me work out my feelings.
> I cried myself to sleep every night.[46]

Herman's case is an example drawn from the 1970s. The following case, from a large western Canadian city in mid-1983,
illustrates how far attitudes and treatment have to go:

> Margaret, living in a one-parent family, was a lonely,
> isolated child. She had few friends, and wasn't close to
> her mother. When she was eleven a neighbour and family
> friend sexually assaulted and finally raped her over a
> period of months. This precipitated a crisis of with-
> drawal, moodiness, crying and wandering from home, but she
> was not able at that time to reveal the sexual abuse. Her
> exasperated mother sent her to stay with her father in
> another Province for a time. In this man's house she was
> further sexually abused. On return to her mother's house
> she was again in conflict with her mother, and finally
> took off at the age of 13. She was soon recruited on the

streets by a leading pimp, and for two years was a very
high-priced juvenile prostitute. She gained nothing from
this experience except grief and further self-disgust.
She was admitted to hospital after a drug overdose, and
then went to a group home as a temporary ward of the
Province. In the group home she was able to reveal for the
first time the earlier sexual assaults on her by her
father and the family friend. The only person she felt
able to talk to was a sympathetic but untrained aide in
the group home. The so-called professionals in the home,
as well as her social worker, agreed to 'let sleeping dogs
lie,' hoping that she had blanked out her traumatic past.
She entered a very withdrawn phase, and her reluctance to
talk about things again was taken as an acquiescence in
this denial. As one of her workers put it, 'Even if we
wanted to refer her for therapy, there's nowhere in this
city we could send her.' Margaret was returned to her
mother since the Province no longer held any legal responsibility for her, now she was 16. It is not clear what
happened between her and her mother, but after two months
she was admitted to hospital after a serious suicide attempt. She has been diagnosed as borderline psychotic, and
in her acutely withdrawn and depressed state has been, at
the age of 16, in a mental hospital for the past two
months. She is being treated with psychotropic drugs, and
still no one has offered her any therapeutic program which
might exorcise this terrible ghost from her past. She remains in a permanent state of self-disgust. The best she
can achieve is a state of numbness, and detachment from
herself, 'like when I was doing tricks. I used to pretend
I was on the wall like a fly or a bird, and then I would
fly away into the sky...'

An Integrated Approach
How could this disastrous outcome for Margaret have been
prevented? In an ideal community she would have known about
the nature of sexual abuse, and would have been able if not
to resist the initial threats and coercion then at least to
report the abuse promptly, with the confidence that speedy
and effective action would be taken. That action would have
removed the source of the abuse, but would not have required
her to endure gruelling cross-examination in court. A humane
approach used in some judicial systems is to permit a social
worker who has interviewed the child to give evidence in
court as a proxy for the victim.

Let's suppose Margaret had been able to reveal the second incident of abuse, when she was 13, to someone like a teacher. In an integrated treatment system a protection worker would have been informed immediately and would have ensured the girl's safety needs by removing the offender from the house. In a community model such as the one developed by Giarretto in San Jose, prosecutors would build on community sentiment supporting an integrated treatment programme. In the face of such pressure, the offender would likely plead guilty in return for a suspended sentence. An intensive programme of therapy would then begin, involving first of all individual treatment of the victim aimed at:

1. Validating the child's experience and the resulting feelings as important and not atypical. Confused feelings of hatred towards those whom we are supposed to love are normal in such a situation.

2. Alleviating the child's guilt feelings: victims frequently hold themselves responsible for the abuse, and their guilt is intensified upon disclosure and the ensuing family disruption.

3. Exploration of the child's feelings towards individual family members, particularly ambiguous feelings towards mother and siblings.

4. Exploration of the child's perception of feelings of other family members towards her. The initial goal is to concentrate on increasing self-awareness and self-esteem in the victim, before she joins groups of victims, and/or begins joint sessions with her mother.

The mother, the most forgotten person in the treatment process, needs counselling too. She needs to know the course treatment will take and its implications; she needs to ventilate and explore her feelings; and her feelings of guilt and shame need to be unburdened. Her own childhood history and feelings about sexuality need to be explored, too, before she can play an active part in treatment and self-help groups.

The adult male must be helped to accept responsibility for the sexual abuse, not only in a legal sense, but in an emotional and moral sense as well. In order to achieve this, the focus has to be on the personality, feelings and childhood of the offender rather than on the offence itself. This is an essential prerequisite for dyadic counselling in which adult and victim will eventually talk to one another frankly: the offender tells the victim why he abused her, and accepts that the responsibility is entirely his. The child herself, in being able to forgive the adult family member,

has then reached an important stage in recovering self-
respect and divesting herself of hatred, both external and
internal. Other important dyads include mother-victim and
mother-father. Family therapy in a group is not an integral
part of this process, and traditional family therapy which
includes both offender and victim from the outset has been
singularly unsuccessful in meeting the victim's needs.47

Finally, the two self-help groups, Parents United and
Daughters and Sons United, provide an important point of
community contact and community education, as well as continued peer support for victims. They represent an important
long-term component of treatment.

It will be clear that a single case of sexual abuse will
occupy many hours of the time of several therapists, whose
work must be coordinated with the activities of other professionals, such as protection workers and police, who will
also be involved. All of this poses a dilemma for child welfare agencies and their budgets. Adequately treating victims
in a way that can restore adequate mental health is complex
and expensive, and requires considerable reorientations of
roles, values, resources, and practice. Social service delivery systems have been extremely reluctant to countenance
such changes. It can be argued that expenditure of time,
energy and resources now will save a great deal in the long
run by reducing the need to institutionalize victims, and
will help to restore mental health to the existing victims.
However, such arguments have failed to convince child welfare authorities of the need for or the possibilities of
change. Unfortunately, in times of 'restraint,' welfare
bureaucracies are rarely open to appeals or arguments even
on grounds of cost benefits, efficiency, rationality or
humanity.

A major thrust is therefore necessary to bring about value
changes which will not only reorder services and expendi-
tures for the treatment of victims in the short run but will
also in the long run prevent the sexual abuse of children.
One way of helping this happen is through educational programmes that tell children what sexual abuse is, how to
resist it and how to report it; operating concurrently with
such programmes would be a widely publicized 'open line'
which kids could ring to get help about sexual abuse.

In the face of professional weakness, lassitude and denial, the initiative has to be taken by victims themselves. A
growing movement of private agencies using Giarretto's
humanistic models and methods has given rise to dynamic and
effective self-help groups of former victims. In the course

of time, these volunteer groups can offer their own open
line, and can bring increasing pressure for change upon in-
transigent social service delivery systems.[48]
   An immediate practical concern regarding adequate referral
and treatment is that all those who have contact with young
people in a professional or volunteer capacity be aware of
the possibility that sexual abuse underlies current distress
or disturbed behaviour. In every such case the question 'Are
you currently being abused by anyone?' should be asked. For
most young people the question will be meaningless, but for
a critical minority the answer will be crucially important.

Conclusions and Summary

Sexual abuse of children in a family context is much more
widespread than was previously thought; moreover, such abuse
frequently has devastating consequences for victims, which
can permanently impair mental health and adjustment if
treatment is absent or inadequate.
   Family sexual abuse of children should be clearly distinguished from incest, which involves adults rather than children. Sexual abuse is supported by a deep-rooted value principle which allows the exploitation of weak and powerless
people, particularly female children. Socialization for
sexual subordination in childhood is an aspect of the general subordination of women. This general value principle allows ego-weak men semblances of power which they exercise
over the most vulnerable members of their families with
relative impunity. Fundamental changes in societal values
are essential to enable victims to reveal abuse and to obtain effective help from adults; such value changes are also
essential if educational programs designed to prevent sexual
abuse of children are to develop effectively. We have argued
that child welfare authorities themselves are generally cau-
tious and conservative in this area. Former victims themselves must therefore lead a community-based movement for
the development of open and comprehensive counselling and
help services which can reach all those currently being
abused, in addition to teaching former victims who suffer
impaired mental health as a result of earlier abuse.

References

   1. B. Morse, 'Native and Métis Children in Canada: victims
      of the child welfare system' in G. Verma and C. Bagley

(Eds) *Race relations and cultural differences: educational and cultural perspectives*. London: Croom-Helm, 1983

2. C. Bagley, 'Bases for the prevention of suicidal behaviour in young people in Alberta,' paper given to the First Annual Symposium on Suicide Research, Calgary, May 1981

3. C. Bagley, 'Incest behaviour and incest taboo,' *Social Problems*, 1969, 16, 505–519; and P. Van Den Berghe, 'Human inbreeding avoidance: culture in nature,' Behavioral and Brain Sciences, 1983, 6, 91–123

4. K. Meiselman, *Incest*. San Francisco: Jossey-Bass, 1978; and B. Schlesinger, Sexual abuse of children. Toronto: University of Toronto Press, 1982

5. J. Goodwin, T. McCarthy and P. DiVasto, 'Prior incest in mothers of abused children,' *Child Abuse and Neglect*, 1981, 5, 87–95

6. J. Herman and L. Hirschman, *Father-daughter incest*. Cambridge, Mass: Harvard University Press, 1981

7. F. Rush, *The best kept secret: sexual abuse of children*. New York: McGraw-Hill, 1980

8. B. Taylor (Ed), *Perspectives on paedophilia*. London: Batsford Academic, 1981

9. R. Bixler, 'The multiple meanings of "incest,"' *Journal of Sex Research*, 1983, 19, 197–201. See also reference 6

10. N. Frude, 'The sexual nature of sexual abuse: a review of the literature,' *Child Abuse and Neglect*, 1982, 6, 211–223

11. J. Peters, 'Children who are victims of sexual assault and the psychology of offenders,' *American Journal of Psychotherapy*, 1976, 398–421

12. S. Butler, *Conspiracy of silence: the trauma of incest*. San Francisco: New Glide Publications

13. E. Sarafino, 'An estimate of nationwide incidence of sexual offenses against children,' *Child Welfare*, 1979, 58, 127–134

14. D. Finkelhor, 'Sexual victimization of children in a normal population,' paper given to Second International Congress on Child Abuse and Neglect, London, September, 1978

15. D. Finkelhor, *Sexually victimized children*. New York Free Press, 1979. See also reference 20

16. D. Finkelhor, 'Public knowledge and attitudes about child sexual abuse: a Boston survey,' paper VS-17 of the Family Violence Research Program, University of New Hampshire, 1980

48   Chris Bagley

17. H. Giarretto, 'The humanistic treatment of child sexual abuse,' paper given to the International Conference on Disturbed Youth, Montreal, May 1983
18. L. Wolfe, *The Cosmo Report*. New York: Arbor House, 1981
19. D. Finkelhor, *Child sexual abuse in a sample of Boston families*. Document No US18S of the Family Violence Research Program, Univesity of New Hampshire, 1982
20. D. Russell, 'The incidence and prevalence of intra-familial and extrafamilial sexual abuse of female children,' *Child Abuse and Neglect*, 1983, 7, 133-146
21. R. Badgley, Committee on Sexual Offenses Against Children and Youth. *Personal Communication*, Toronto, June 1982
22. M. Tsai, S. Feldman-Summers and M. Edgar, 'Childhood molestation: variables related to differential impacts on psychosexual functioning in adult women,' *Journal of Abnormal Psychology*, 1979, 88, 401-417
23. See 4
24. L. Schultz (Ed), *The sexual victimology of youth*. Springfield, Ill: Charles C. Thomas, 1980
25. J. Denward and J. Densen-Gerber, 'Incest as a causative factor in antisocial behavior: an exploratory study,' *Contemporary Drug Problems*, 1975, 4, 323-340
26. J. James and J. Meyerding, 'Early sexual experience and prostitution,' *American Journal of Psychiatry*, 1977, 134, 1381-1385
27. L. Anderson, 'Notes on the linkage between the sexually abused child and the suicidal adolescent,' *Journal of Adolescence*, 1982, 5; and C. Bagley, 'Adult mental health sequels of family child sexual abuse,' paper given to Annual meeting of the American Association for the Study of Social Problems, Detroit, September 1983
28. M. Silbert and A. Piven, 'Sexual abuse as an antecedent to prostitution,' *Child Abuse and Neglect*, 1981, 5, 407-411
29. C. Bagley, 'Child sexual abuse and childhood sexuality: a review of the monograph literature 1978 to 1982,' *Journal of Child Care*, 1982, 2, 100-121
30. D. Finkelhor, 'Sexual abuse: a sociological perspective,' paper given to Third International Congress of Child Abuse and Neglect, Amsterdam, April 1981
31. P. Skolseg, 'Social service coordination of treatment of victims of child sexual abuse,' *Child Welfare Forum*, 1983, 2,
32. D. Finkelhor, 'Risk factors in the sexual victimization of youth,' *Child Abuse and Neglect*, 1980, 4, 265-273

33. See 7
34. S. Forward and C. Buck, *Betrayal of innocence: incest and its devastations*. Toronto: MacMillan, 1978
35. S. Hill, 'Child sexual abuse: selected issues,' M.S.W. Thesis, University of Calgary, 1982
36. C. Bagley, 'Child sexual abuse: annotated bibliography of the journal literature, 1978 to 1982,' *Journal of Child Care*, 1983, 4
37. D. Finkelhor, 'What's wrong with sex between adults and children? Ethics and the problem of sexual abuse,' *American Journal of Orthopsychiatry*, 1979, 49, 692–697
38. H. Cohen, *Equal rights for children*. New York: Little Field Adams
39. See 15
40. A. Maslow, *Dominance, self-esteem and self-actualization*. California: Brooks–Cole, 1973
41. L. Sanford, *The silent children: a parent's guide to the prevention of child sexual abuse*. New York: Anchor Press, 1970
42. C. Adams and J. Fay, *No more secrets: protecting your child from sexual assault*. San Luis Obispo, Ca: Impact Publishers, 1981; and B. and R. Justice, *The broken taboo: sex in the family*. New York: Human Sciences Press, 1979
43. S. Sgroi (Ed), *Handbook of clinical intervention in child sexual abuse*. Lexington, Mass: Lexington Books, 1982
44. H. Giarretto, *Integrated treatment of child sexual abuse: a treatment and training manual*. Palo Alto, Ca: Science and Behavior Books, Inc., 1982. On the adaptation of this approach to meet the needs of a Canadian community, see: C. Anderson and P. Mayes, 'Treating family sexual abuse: the humanistic approach,' *Journal of Child Care*, 1982, 2, 31–47
45. On intervention and therapy with male victims, see C. Linedecker, *Children in Chains*. New York: Everest House, 1981; see also reference 24
46. J. Herman and L. Hirschman, *Father-daughter incest*. Cambridge, Mass: Harvard University Press, 1981. See also D. Finkelhor, 'Removing the child – prosecuting the offender in cases of sexual abuse: evidence from the national reporting system for child abuse and neglect,' *Child Abuse and Neglect*, 1983, 7, 195–205
47. H. Giarretto, 'A comprehensive child sexual abuse treatment program,' *Child Abuse and Neglect*, 1982, 6, 263–278. Group treatment of victims alone can, however, be highly effective. See reference 34

50   Chris Bagley

48. C. Bagley, 'The gentle revolution,' *Starting Over:
    Newsletter of Sons and Daughters United*, Calgary Chapter
    (P.O. Box 1161, Station J, Calgary, Alberta, 403-242-
    8529), April 1982. In Calgary, Giarretto's approach has
    been adapted by Anderson and Mayes to suit local needs –
    see reference 42

Reprinted with permission from *Canada's Mental Health*, June
1984, Vol 32, No 2. Health Services and Promotion Branch,
Mental Health Division, Health and Welfare, Canada.

# 4. GUIDELINES FOR INVESTIGATIVE INTERVIEWING OF CHILD VICTIMS OF SEXUAL ABUSE

MARY WELLS

## Foreword

These guidelines were originally prepared as a discussion paper at an interdisciplinary training session to inaugurate the *Child Sexual Abuse Protocol* in Metropolitan Toronto. They have been revised following consultation with police, child welfare social workers and the Crown Attorney's Office.

These guidelines cover a number of areas considered to be of key importance in conducting an investigative interview, including:

- Feelings – the child's/the interviewer's
- Checklist
- Preparing for the interview
- Seating arrangements
- Establishing trust
- A neutral location
- Background information
- Getting started
- Children's sense of time
- Children's language
- Use of aids: drawings, dolls
- Validating the child's credibility
- Concluding the interview

It is possible to obtain complete information even from reluctant children, very young children and children with poor verbal or mental ability. Keep in mind that the child's anxiety may be acting as a block. Move in a gentle but firm progression from less sensitive to more sensitive areas. Move on as you sense the child becoming more comfortable with you. Listen carefully, encouarge the child to continue until she and you are sure you have the whole story. Do not

make promises or ask leading questions. Aids such as drawings and dolls can be invaluable for depicting what children
are unable to express verbally. Verbal labels can then be
attached to what the child has depicted or demonstrated.
Conclude the interview carefully, letting the child know she
has done very hard work. Give her as much information as
possible and let her know that your interest will continue
and she will be cared for.

The author wishes to acknowledge the contributions of numerous professionals who freely shared both their successes
and failures so that we could all benefit. Thanks also to
Lorna Grant for her advice and editorial eye.

Finally, and most importantly, this paper is dedicated to
Kim, June, Pauline, Maureen, Janice, Liz, Jean, Gord, and
the many others whose courage and perseverance have inspired
all of us. They serve as constant reminders that, together,
we can stop hurting.

Introduction

These guidelines have been prepared to assist child welfare
and police personnel conducting an initial investigative interview of a child where there has been an allegation of
child sexual abuse. They are designed for use in conjunction
with the *Child Sexual Abuse Protocol*, which outlines a coordinated community approach now being implemented in Metropolitan Toronto. These guidelines will facilitate an in-
depth interview by professionals with a mandated responsibility to conduct investigations. Professionals (such as
teachers, public health nurses and so on) who are mandated
to *report* child abuse should not undertake an investigative
interview. They should refer instead to 'Talking to the
Child Who May Have Been Sexually Abused – Suggestions for
Reporting Professionals.'[1]

It should be kept in mind that the methods described on
the following pages have proven both practical and effective. Suggestions apply, in most respects, to all age groups
and can prove useful in interviewing even very young or
handicapped children with poor verbal skills. However, each
child and each situation will present unique features. Interviewers should feel free to adapt and respond in ways
they feel are appropriate for the circumstances.

The goals of the investigative interview are to: (a) assure protection of the child, and (b) determine whether an
offence has occurred. Whenever possible, the interview

should be tape-recorded to avoid the necessity of interviewing the child again later. A sexually abused child will
likely be highly anxious at the prospect of talking about
the details of the abuse. Prolonging the disclosure over
more than one interview can increase the anxiety further.
The child is likely to talk more spontaneously at the time
of the crisis than she will later. Therefore, the first interview of the child should be comprehensive and aimed towards gathering all information immediately required.

A number of factors should be considered in interviewing
the child. Perhaps among the most important are the knowledge and experience of the investigators. Children reporting sexual abuse should be presumed to be telling the truth.
Every report warrants a full investigation, even in the face
of initial denial by one or more of the individuals. False
denials of sexual abuse are more common than false reports.[2]

In these guidelines, the victim is referred to as 'she'
and the offender as 'he,' reflecting current occurrence
statistics.

Feelings - The Child's/The Interviewer's

The Child's
When it has just been disclosed that a child has been the
victim of sexual abuse, the child experiences a new crisis
in life. That which has been previously a secret now has
come out into the open. The child's feelings of shame,
guilt, anxiety, fear and confusion are exposed for the first
time to adults who are outside the abusive relationship and
outside the child's family. The child wonders if she will be
believed, wonders if people will be angry, disappointed or
rejecting of her. It is possible that she may not have de-
liberately disclosed that she has been sexually abused. If
this is the case, she may be reluctant to talk and fearful
of the implications. The child may have been bribed, coerced
or threatened into maintaining the secret. It is common for
abusers to tell the child she is responsible for the abuse,
that if she tells anyone she may be responsible for the
abuser going to jail, the breakup of the family. She may
have been told that her mother will have a nervous breakdown
or no one will believe her is she discloses.

The Interviewer's
Even experienced investigators may experience a sense of
shock, revulsion or outrage at the offender. The child,

however, may not be feeling that way at all. If the child senses a horrified response from the adult, it communicates to the child that she has been involved in something of which she should be ashamed. This has the effect of increasing the trauma the child has already experienced. While it is critical that the interviewers be both self-aware and empathetic, they should not convey their own feelings to the child. Rather, they should be encouraging and supportive, but neutral.

Checklist

Interviewers should asses the child's level of maturity and understanding of sexuality and functions of various body parts in securing the following information during the first interview:
- chronological age
- family relationships
- cultural/social background
- name of the offender; his present location
- the relationship of the child to the offender
- the duration and extent of the abuse
- what happened *in detail*, when it happened, where, and how often
- date/time of last occurrence; likelihood of physical evidence
- names of anyone else having knowledge of the abuse
- names of anyone else involved in or observing the abuse
- whether the child has been bribed, threatened and/or physically harmed at any time
- whether the child has been bribed or threatened to either (a) take part in the activity or (b) keep the activity secret
- names of anyone the child has told in the past and what happened
- if the child has not told the non-offending parent(s), is she able to say why
- child's assessment of current situation and what should happen next, eg, does she have support; is she safe at home, etc.

Preparing for the Interview

Interviewing a child is considerably different than interviewing an adult. Children are less verbal than adults and often communicate non-verbally through their behaviour, play

or art. If there will be two interviewers (such as a police/
child welfare team), they should decide in advance who will
take the lead and adopt the primary interviewing role. The
interview should take place in a neutral location, if possible away from where the alleged abuse occurred.[3]

The interviewers should arrange seating in as non-
threatening a manner as possible. Do not tower over the
child. Try to avoid having two adults confronting the child
face-to-face. Instead, try having the interviewers sitting
on either side of the child or one interviewer facing the
child, one sitting beside the child. The child should be
asked if she wants anyone else present (for example, her
mother). If she requests this, the person should sit behind
the child, out of the child's direct view.

Begin the interview armed with as much information as you
can obtain. It helps to know the child's name, nickname,
parents' names, brothers' and sisters' names, pets if any,
name of the child's school, teacher, grade. Attempt to obtain any other relevant information that may colour the
child's response: is she mentally or physically handicapped,
has she been sick recently, has there been any recent trauma
in the family (death, divorce, moves, etc.) - and so on. It
is also important to know as much as possible about the circumstances leading up to the disclosure of abuse.

Obtaining the Child's Statement

Keep in mind at all times that you may not suggest what may
have happened or ask the child leading questions. You must
never offer a reward for talking or a threat of retribution
if she does not talk. Children respond better when you go
from the general to the specific and from the less sensitive
to the more sensitive areas in a gentle but persistent progression.

Getting Started

Tell the child your name(s) and what your jobs are (ie,
police officer, social worker). Tell the child that your job
is to help children who may be having a problem. Tell the
child that you have been told that she has been having a
problem and you need to talk with her. Tell the child she
can help you to do your job is she will talk with you now.
(Children often respond well to a request to help an adult.)

At this point, introduce the audio-tape. Tell the child it
helps you to do your job if you can put your talk with the

child onto tape. Show the child how the machine works and allow her to play with it. Start the tape, play it back, allow the child to talk into it, then say you are going to start the tape so that from now on, everything everyone says can be recorded. Tell the child everything now will be recorded so everyone should leave the tape alone.

(You may find, however, that the child will want to periodically speak or sing into the microphone. Permit this for a minute or so as long as the tape is not turned off. Children do this kind of thing to discharge anxiety.) If you let them play a little it will reduce their anxiety. *Do not get into a power struggle with the child over the tape recorder!*

Establish the purpose of the interview by saying that 'We have been told that something has been happening to you that you don't feel quite right about. We have been told you have been having a problem with (name alleged offender) and we would like you to talk about it.' Then return to the concrete information that is non-threatening. For example, ask the child if she remembers the day about which you have information. Ask if something happened, can the child talk about it. Say that it's important to talk if something happened and it's okay to talk. Tell the child that the interviewers have talked with lots of children – and that if something has happened, the interviewers can help, but they need to hear from the child first.

## Children's Sense of Time

Children do not relate to time the way adults do by referring to dates, hours, etc. Rather, they relate to birthdays, holidays, seasons, night and day, special events or the time certain shows are on television. Ask the child where the child was when the alleged incident occurred, who else was present, who else may have been nearby. Ask the child if she remembers if it was a school day or a holiday. Ask when she got up, what did she have for breakfast, what did she wear, what was the weather like, did she go out of the house, what did she do, did she come back to the house, etc. Lead the questions toward the time of the alleged incident.

## Children's Language

Allow the child to tell the story in her own words. Young children may know only slang words for parts of their bodies and may be embarrassed to say them. Tell the child that her own words are okay. Adolescents may use formal or technical words. Ask questions to assure yourself that you and they understand the same meaning for the words. (For example, if an adolescent says 'make love,' do not assume she means vaginal intercourse. Ask them precisely what happened in terms of placement of hands, penis, vagina, enlargement of penis, semen emerging and so on.)

When the child talks, nod your head and repeat the words the child is using. When the child pauses, help her to continue talking by saying 'and then what happened.' You may say something like 'You have told me he touched you, can you show me where he touched you?' Only after the child has begun talking and is describing an incident, should you press for clarification of details: 'Where were his hands, where were your hands?' 'Were your clothes on, were his clothes on, who took them off?' 'Was he saying anything, what was he saying?' Let the child know she is doing well by giving you complete information. If she is showing distress, let her know that you know she is upset, that you understand how hard this is, but it is a good thing to talk about it. Do not ask directive questions or questions that suggest a response such as 'Did he touch you on the breast?' This must be volunteered by the child. Such information must emanate from the child, *not* the interviewer.

## Use of Aids

### Drawings

Some children may respond better if they are given an opportunity to express themselves in drawings before they have to commit themselves with words. If possible, drawing materials should be out on the table before the interview begins. The child may initiate drawing. If the child is not talking or drawing, one of the interviewers can take pen and paper (bright coloured felt pens or crayons are ideal) and begin drawing. Stick to the concept of beginning with less threatening matters. The interviewer could draw herself, the police station, the school, the neighbourhood. Draw a picture of the interviewer talking to the child. Leave the faces blank, invite the child to fill in the faces. Encourage the child to take over the drawing. Respond to the kind of expression you see. For example, as 'Is that a sad face? Is this an angry face?,' then ask the child to draw her house, brothers, sisters, mother, father, the alleged

offender (if it is not the father), ask the child to tell
you their names, to describe the expressions on their
faces. It can be helpful to assist the child in drawing a
diagram of her house or wherever the abuse occurred. This
can be used to clarify location of the abuse, sequence of
events, location of other persons at the time of the abuse.

## Dolls

Anatomically-complete dolls can be a useful tool in interviewing a sexually abused child. They may be used to help a
silent child talk or they may be used to clarify information
the child has given you verbally.

If you have dolls, have them in view, fully clothed, before you begin the interview. You may introduce the dolls by
either pointing to them or holding them in your lap. If you
are holding the dolls, try to remember that the dolls sym-
bolize the child. They should be held gently, in a cuddling
fashion. If you are not comfortable holding dolls, leave
them in a chair or sitting close together on a shelf. Tell
the child the dolls are special because they have all their
body parts. Tell the child she can look at them or undress
them if she wishes.

Allow the child to approach the dolls. Do not hand the
dolls to the child. It works much better if the child initi-
ates handling the dolls. If the child does not want to
handle the dolls, tell the child that it is okay and go back
to drawing.

If the child wishes to use the dolls, allow her to explore
the dolls for a few minutes with no comment on your part except approving nods, etc. The child may show embarrassment,
laughter at the genitals. You could ask the child what she
calls the body parts as she comments or touches the penis,
vagina, rectum, etc.

Ask the child if she knows which is the girl doll, the boy
doll, the woman doll, the man doll. Ask how she knows. (She
will likely point out the obvious differences.) If the child
has been abused, she may demonstrate aggression between the
dolls by hitting them against each other or throwing them
around. Make comments on what you are seeing: 'He's hitting
her, she's beating him up.' (Sometimes abused children will
symbolically beat their abuser by making the child doll beat
the adult doll.)

The child may depict sexual acts in the doll play by
putting one doll on top of another and making the dolls

simulate sexual activity. Tell the child what you see she
has the doll doing, 'The man doll is on top, the girl doll
is on the bottom, they are doing something. What are they
doing? Can you tell me?' Do not interpret beyond this point,
rather, ask the child if anything more is happening. If the
child tells you or shows you more, keep listening and asking
about more until the child says that is all.

Then ask the child if she knows any names to describe what
she has been showing you. 'Does the girl doll have names for
it, does the man doll have names for it?' 'What does the man
doll say while it is happening, what does the girl doll
say?' Ask if there are other people around, for example,
'Where is the Mummy doll?' *Ask the child if she has seen
this happen, and if she has, to whom it has happened.* If she
says it has happened to herself, ask who was the offender
('person doing these things'), and then begin questioning
about time, locations, frequency. The child will likely continue to play with the dolls and may attempt to head the
conversation off topic. Allow her to play, tell her she is
doing a good job, you know it is hard and she needs to help
you by talking a little more until you are finished.

The dolls should be reclothed and put back in their places
before the child leaves the room. The child may do this or
you may help her. This activity symbolically tells the child
that what she has shown you and spoken about are finished,
the lid is back on and she does not need to talk anymore.

## Validating the Child's Credibility

A useful framework for validating the child's complaint has
been developed by Dr. Susan Sgroi who has found that the
presence of certain characteristics tend to enhance the
credibility of the child's story:
1. The presence of multiple incidents occurring over time.
2. Progression of sexual activity from less intimate to
   more intimate types of interaction.
3. Elements of secrecy.
4. Elements of pressure or coercion.
5. The child should be able to give explicit details of the
   sexual behaviour. When establishing the criteria, the
   interviewer must review the methodology used in the interview and be satisfied that the methods used were con-
   ducive to allowing the child to articulate this information.[4]

## Concluding the Interview

A child disclosing sexual abuse has usually revealed her
deepest, most confusing and frightening thoughts. The child
needs praise, reassurance, protection. Give her as much
information as possible about what will happen next. Ask the
child what she would like to see happen next. Try to agree
to one request (ie, let her talk to her mother, have a
drink, have something to eat, etc.).

You may wish to briefly explain to the child that what the
person did to her is against the law and the police may lay
charges against the person involved. If she asks if the person will go to jail, tell her that sometimes happens, but
that the decision on that is up to a judge, and everyone involved would like to see the person get help so he stops doing these things.

Tell the child that you will be staying in touch and keeping an eye on her to be sure she is all right.

As the interview ends, you may be entrusting the child to
another adult. (It may be a non-offending parent or it may
be someone else.) Tell the person in front of the child that
the child has done very hard work, you are pleased with her,
that she is probably very tired. If you will be interviewing
the child again, tell her so and give her an idea of when it
may take place.

## A Final Word to Interviewers

A children's therapist who was herself a victim of sexual
abuse for many years as a young child has said that she
wishes someone had given her the opportunity to 'tell' when
she was a child. She recalls looking at a teacher and
wondering if she could tell this person but never had an
opening she could use. Children need adults to listen to
them carefully and seriously. Sometimes they need adults to
help them express things that are very difficult to articulate.

These guidelines have been prepared in the hope that
children will be protected from further abuse as more professionals become skilled in conducting investigative interviews.

The gentle but persistent progression outlined in these
guidelines has proven to be a helpful method in assisting
children to disclose the secret of child sexual abuse.

Notes

1. 'Talking to the Child Who May Have Been Sexually Abused
   – Suggestions for Reporting Professionals.' The
   Metropolitan Chairman's Special Committee on Child
   Abuse, September 1983
2. *Child Sexual Abuse Protocol*. The Metropolitan Chairman's
   Special Committee on Child Abuse, November 1983, pp IV,
   V
3. *Child Sexual Abuse Protocol*, p 4
4. Sgroi, Suzanne M., *Handbook of Clinical Intervention in
   Child Sexual Abuse*. Toronto: D.C. Heath and Company,
   Lexington Books, 1982, pp 71–73

Reprinted with permission from the Metropolitan Chairman's
Special Committee on Child Abuse, Toronto, Ontario, Canada,
1984.

5. THE ROLE OF A RURAL TEAM IN PREVENTING SEXUAL ABUSE OF
   CHILDREN: A SUMMARY

   ERIC SIGURDSON AND MALCOLM STRANG

Historically, society has changed existing patterns of abnormal behaviour. Slavery, a form of abuse, existed as one
group had power and authority over another, and changed when
that authority was removed by society. Child work laws, and
legislation requiring basic education for all children has,
in the last 150 years, given children power.
  Children lack power or authority when they are exposed to
potential sexual abuse. Prevention includes increasing children's awareness of their rights, and in enacting legislation to guarantee these rights, obligating caregivers to
protect and educate them.
  Physical abuse has been recognized as a major health problem. The 'battered baby syndrome' is known to most health
workers. Less is known about sexual abuse and there is less
support for those who attempt to identify it. This will
change as public education is introduced into society.
  In the last 10 years there has been an increasing awareness of sexual abuse of children. Child sexual abuse is a
wide range of abnormal sexual behaviour, involving a child
and an older caregiver. It includes exploiting a child for
the gratification of the parent or caregiver, sexual molestation, sexual assault, child pornography and child prostitution; it is not restricted to incest. This behaviour
occurs much more frequently than is generally reported.
Steps to deal with sexual abuse include recognizing and
documenting abusive behaviour as a beginning to a programme
of prevention.
  Such steps have been taken by the Suspected Child Abuse
and Neglect Team (SCAN) in Dauphin, Manitoba. The Team's
formation and operation are discussed in an earlier article,
which is available upon request.

The Dauphin SCAN Team intervened in 22 cases between July 1980 and December 1982. We have reviewed each case under the following headings: presentation, resolution and preventive steps taken. Space limitations prevent the publication of the details associated with the 22 cases. These details in the full article are available from the authors.

However, some important findings were: family doctors and police are important sources of referral; vaginal intercourse accounted for half the cases; the offender was a male 'friend' in nearly half the cases.

The case distribution was fairly even across the district; 8 cases in towns, 10 in communities less than 500 people, 4 on reserves. Twelve of the 22 cases had serious complications, including gonorrhea, vaginal injuries and pregnancy.

In 7 cases children were removed termporarily and in 3 cases permanently.

Community awareness was used to provide a protective response in 18 cases, 6 cases proceeded to criminal court; many others didn't for lack of corroborative evidence.

Twenty-one girls and 1 boy were abused. The age range was 3 to 17 years. The average age was 9.16 years.

Prevention was considered possible in 19 cases, 14 cases continued to be monitored.

How Can Sexual Abuse of Children be Prevented?

All the offenders in our study were male. Common to them were some or all of the following: unemployment, alcoholism, sexual aggression, and a dependent personality. Often their wives, or common-law wives, were self-demeaning and lacked authority. The child was an innocent party in this relationship. The sexual abuse was a family secret.

Prevention is difficult but possible through early intervention with children. Prevention can be primary, secondary or tertiary, and preventive steps are based on the following observations.

Primary Prevention
Primary prevention discourages disease from developing or an injury from occurring. Educating adults and children about normal and abnormal sexual behaviour is a cornerstone in a programme to prevent sexual abuse of children. Healthy sexual behaviour should be recognized. Education and family life should emphasize normal behaviour, and recognize and

deal with abnormal sexual behaviour. This education certainly should begin before young people become parents. Prenatal classes are important to prepare both partners for the inevitable frustrations of childbearing.

Legislation can be an effective tool in the primary prevention of many conditions. A school curriculum that requires education about normal and abnormal sexual behaviour, will give children the knowledge and confidence to say, 'NO' to potential abusers.

## Secondary Prevention

Secondary prevention means early detection and intervention, preferably before the condition is clinically apparent; it means to reverse, halt or at least slow a condition's progress. Children who have been abused are more likely to repeat the pattern of behaviour when they are parents. Recognizing this, establishing a high risk registry, and offering an active treatment programme are important steps to secondary prevention. It is also vital to listen carefully to children and be aware of the warning signs of sexual abuse. If sexual abuse is detected early less damage is likely to occur.

## Tertiary Prevention

Tertiary prevention means minimizing the effects of disease and disability, by surveillance and maintenance aimed at preventing complications and premature deterioration.

The offender, in cases of sexual abuse, is like an alcoholic; once the abuse has occurred it may recur. The risk is always there. This life long risk is an important factor in sexual abuse. Studies have shown that in cases of physical abuse, the offender often had a history of being abused as a child. This is likely true in cases of sexual abuse.

Family therapy sessions with the victim and offender help to prevent and ameliorate further psychological damage from sexual abuse. Unfortunately, there are limited resources for this important aspect of prevention, especially in a rural setting. The preventive steps taken in the 22 cases are mainly tertiary. The SCAN Team is now planning to emphasize primary and secondary prevention.

## Conclusion

Our local experience suggests a program of primary, secondary and tertiary prevention is a viable way to prevent and

treat sexual abuse. Society must begin to combat sexual
abuse with these three types of prevention.

Prevention is the most difficult and most important aspect
of ending sexual abuse. It is generally agreed that sexual
abuse occurs far more frequently than is reported. A prevention programme based on primary, secondary and tertiary prevention is possible and highly desirable. Community awareness
and education have been effective in stopping known sexual
abuse and appear to have significant potential to prevent new
episodes. An interdisciplinary team approach facilitates the
development of this program.

Copies of the full article, on which this summary is based,
are available from the authors at 15 - 1st Avenue, SW, Dauphin,
Manitoba R7N 1R9.

Reprinted with permission from the *Manitoba Social Worker*,
January 1985, Vol 19, No 1. Manitoba Association of Social
Workers, 1985.

6. THERAPEUTIC VALUE OF SELF-HELP GROUPS FOR SEXUAL ABUSE VICTIMS

LINDA HALLIDAY

Sexual abuse does not have to bring lifelong devastation to the victim. Psychologists, psychiatrists and therapists can help, but sometimes the people best able to provide a supportive environment to deal with the emotional pain and guilt are fellow victims.

Sexual Abuse Victims Anonymous Society (SAVA) originated from such an idea. SAVA was established in Campbell River, B.C., in 1981 as a self-help group for adults who suffered sexual victimization as children and were unable to deal with the abuse. The group was loosely structured and based on the 12 steps of the Alcoholics Anonymous programme.

As a sexual abuse victim myself, I led the group of four women who ranged in age from 22 to 35. We met weekly in an atmosphere characterized initially by a lack of trust and inhibited discussion.

The AA programme format soon proved impractical. In addition to being too structured, in many cases the programme steps could not be applied to sexual abuse. Asking members to turn their lives over to a 'higher power' was contradictory as the basic purpose of the group was to give victims back control over their own lives.

As well, the AA policy of sponsoring the attendance of others at meetings was not feasible. Visitors – who were there for such reasons as curiosity, support for a friend, or out of ignorance as to what sexual abuse entailed – compromised the confidentiality of group members. We found that a screening process was necessary first and foremost, and some individual counselling required to determine if potential members were ready for the group. This protected group members and eliminated the need for members to bring a friend for support.

A confidentiality contract was also developed. Witnessed
by other members, each new member signed the contract which
provided a 'safety net' for those in the group. While there
are many arguments in opposition to such contracts, it must
be noted that child sexual abuse victims have suffered a
tremendous betrayal of trust. Re-establishing trust is a
most difficult task. The contract afforded some sense of
security to the group.

These women needed that security. One common trait with
all members was emotional immaturity. It appeared these
women had stopped growing emotionally at the approximate
time the abuse became traumatic for them. They had developed
patterns of victimization that followed them well into their
adult relationships.

With time, group members came to feel more comfortable
with each other. Meetings became a safe place to disclose
the psychological damage that had been done to us - not only
by the offender, but by other family members and those we
had trusted enough to confide in. The horror and disbelief
that frequently followed disclosure and the further victimization by those who didn't believe or protect the child
caused damage often as severe as the actual abuse itself.

The group successfully provided the emotional and moral
support needed by victims who were either confronting their
family or offender or who were involved in the legal process. For any self-help group, the support system outside
meetings is vital in developing a strong bond among members.
An exchange of first names and phone numbers is a good step.
As time passes, group members become family to those victims
who have lost their own families as a result of either disclosures or confrontations.

The group members mainly provide support and understanding
while they work on building self-esteem and assertiveness,
overcoming destructive behaviour, learning to take back
their power and control and working toward a more positive
lifestyle. Confrontation and honesty are essential among
members when working within a self-help group.

Members also give each other encouragement and approval
for even the smallest accomplishment. To the 'outside
world,' it may not seem significant that a person had gone
shopping for the first time in two years. For a victim,
telling other group members of this achievement would win
approval as a step to a more positive lifestyle.

In group, the abuse is acknowledged and dealt with but
members are not allowed to use it as a crutch or excuse for

present inappropriate behaviour. Group members are encouraged to begin taking some responsibility for their lives
today. Empathy and understanding are encouraged - sympathy
and pity are not.

As group leader I became a 'safe authority' figure. The
members were given options to different situations they
faced but were forced to make their own decisions and accept the consequences. The group gave support and feedback
for any member making changes or choices, but refused to
make the decision itself or take responsibility for the
success or failure of it.

Gradually members begin to take control over their actions rather than have the abuse control their actions. The
group helps each other let go of the abuse and the offender,
discarding a negative lifestyle and replacing it with positive reinforcement. Members help each other through problems
such as drug abuse, alcohol abuse, battering situations, re-
turning to school, finding a job, and provide moral support
when the step is made to seek professional help. (Members
encourage each other to seek further help if the need
arises.)

A self-help group provides a safe 'dumping ground' for
victims of sexual abuse to rid themselves of the silence and
secrecy that has surrounded them. It renders an atmosphere
which takes away the feelings of isolation and shame that
makes a victim believe they are both at fault and the only
one who was sexually abused.

One problem I have seen arising with self-help groups is
that the 'safe authority' figure becomes a 'power tripper'
and causes further damage to the victim. The group leader
becomes so engrossed in their own power that they uninten-
tionally victimize the victim - by making decisions for
them, passing judgment, taking away their approval, forcing
them to take action for which they are unprepared, keeping
them in the 'victim' role, giving misinformation or dis-
couraging them from seeking additional help.

To prevent this, the group leader must have good counselling skills and not have an ego problem.

A self-help group is not the answer for all who have been
sexually victimized, but can complement other services as
one more rung up the ladder to overcoming the abuse. But
standing alone, without regulations which govern other self-
help groups, they can also be devastating. I recommend that
you check out any self-help groups carefully before referring those who seek help.

SAVA has changed its focus from a self-help group to a provider of information, training and advocacy, crisis counselling, liaison, and referrals. For more information contact the author: Linda Halliday, Sexual Abuse Consultant, 1901 19th Avenue, Campbell River, B.C. V9W 4M7. Telephone: (604) 287-2694 or 287-9118.

Reprinted with permission of the author from *Initiative*, December 1984, Vol 1, No 2. Canadian Council on Social Development, Ottawa, Ontario, Canada.

7. FATHERS ANONYMOUS – A GROUP TREATMENT PROGRAM FOR SEXUAL
   OFFENDERS

ROSS DAWSON

A Growing Problem

Until very recently the sexual abuse of children was a taboo
topic. Public and professional acknowledgment and discussion
of this form of child abuse was avoided or limited. Sexual
abuse of children was described as the 'last frontier' in
our efforts to protect children. This is now changing. Slow-
ly, the veil of secrecy is being lifted and the door of discussion is being opened on this form of child maltreatment.
As a result of changing public attitudes it is now possible
without fear of censure or social repercussion to acknowledge clinically or publically the existence of child sexual
abuse in society, including sexual abuse by members of the
child's family. In addition our increased acceptance of the
existence of family sexual abuse has enabled victims of this
misconduct to seek professional assistance and treatment or
to describe publicly their experience. Autobiographical or
biographical accounts of sexual abuse such as 'Kiss Daddy
Goodnight,'[1] or 'Daddy's Girl'[2] demonstrate this new accept-
ability of public discussion about this social problem.
   This 'new' awareness of sexual abuse has resulted in increased reports of child sexual abuse being made to child
welfare agencies. Reports to the Ontario Child Abuse
Register provide an example of this surge in reporting cases
of sexual abuse of children.

The Reluctance to Provide Treatment

The response of agencies mandated to deal with this increase
in reported incidents of sexual abuse is currently at a very
beginning level. The initial response has generally been
confined to developing identification and and investigation

skills and to providing care and protection for the child
victim. Some innovative treatment approaches have been attempted. However, these have usually focussed on ameliorat-
ing the effects of the sexual abuse upon the child or the
adult who was abused as a child.

No comprehensive treatment approaches offering a variety
of treatment modalities for all family members has emerged
in Canada. Nor have specific treatment programmes been developed which have as their goal the rehabilitation of the
abusing father. Why is this?

At least three reasons can be given to explain the current
lack of therapeutic endeavour:

1. The present limit of knowledge and research: The sexual
abuse of children is a new and emerging field of study. Consequently, our knowledge about sexual abuse, its nature, extent, etiology and consequences is limited and incomplete.
Because our findings are limited and tentative we simply do
not know which treatment approach is most effective with
which families or individuals. If our findings about sexual
abuse are tentative, even more so are our treatment initia-
tives in this area.

2. Professional insecurity: In addition to the present
limitation of knowledge and research, other constraints im-
pinge upon and hinder the treatment of family sexual abuse.
One of the foremost practice constraints is the feeling of
many practitioners that they lack both the·confidence and
competence to provide treatment in cases of sexual abuse.
Perhaps due to the secrecy and taboo which has surrounded
this phenomenon for so long there is a widely held misper-
ception that some esoteric skills or process is necessary
for the treatment of this form of family dysfunction.

3. Conflicting emotions: The sexual abuse of children, and
particularly the family sexual abuse of children generates
strong emotional reactions. The reactions are likely to be
intense and conflicting. Reactions may range from concern to
vengeance or disgust to curiousity. As a result, we are am-
bivalent as to whether our intervention should be therapeutic or punitive. Generally, our most humanistic consideration is given to the sexually misused child, while our most
punitive approach is directed toward the abusing father.
Our feelings towards these fathers are usually characterized
by considerable anger and revenge, both of which block the
development of necessary treatment programmes for these individuals.

The Fathers' Need for Treatment

From the analysis of reported cases of sexual abuse, it is apparent that approximately 85% involve fathers or father figures sexually involved with dependent daughters. Fathers represent the largest perpetrators. If we intend to maintain the family unit or eventually to reunite it, then some rehabilitation efforts must be afforded to the offender.

In most cases of the family sexual misconduct, the child sexually involved with their father does not want to leave home, does not want the father sent to jail or to see the fragmentation of their family. Most of these children experience both positive and negative emotions towards their father. While angry at their abuse they may also have fond memories and experiences in relation to their father. Usually, their disclosure of the sexual misconduct is motivated more by a desire to get treatment for the father than by a determination to see him punished. In fact, many children experience additional feelings of guilt when following disclosure the father is arrested, jailed or punished. All of which contributes to a further traumatization of the child.

Some of the findings to date regarding the common characteristics of the spouses of these fathers suggest they are generally passive and psychologically and financially dependent upon their husband. They tend to preserve their relationship with their husband at all costs. This can be seen in their lack of disclosure of the sexual misconduct, their appearent disbelief of the daughter's story and their willingness to have the daughter leave home in preference to the father's enforced departure. Even where fathers are removed from the family home or are incarcerated, it is a common phenomenon for the couple to reunite. Without treatment the underlying family dynamics may remain unaltered and the potential for further sexual misconduct remains high.

At times it is convenient or reassuring to consider that fathers involved sexually with their daughters are 'sick,' 'mentally ill,' or 'perverted.' The conceptualization of the sexual abuse of children as a sexual problem beloning to a mentally ill father is both simplistic and incorrect. The typical sexually abusive father is not oversexed, psychotic, nor does he have psychotic tendencies. This thinking allows us to view such fathers as a little less than human; dangerous individuals who should be put away. And put away they are. Because of a lack of treatment programmes many fathers are incarcerated, where, during this period of confinement,

they receive no active treatment. Consequently, they return
to their families or establish new families with a high
potential for further incidents of sexual misconduct. Faced
with a conviction under the Criminal Code for a sexual offence and an absence of community treatment programmes,
judges have few alternatives to incarceration for the perpetrator. Despite attempts to stereotype them, most fathers
who have been sexually involved with their daughters have no
previous criminal record or history of deviant behaviour,
are not violent, demonstrate remorse and can be assisted
through a rehabilitative therapeutic approach working in
cooperation with the judicial system.

   While sexual misconduct with a dependent child is wrong,
it is by no means the worst crime perpetrated upon children
by their parents. In fact, the parental breaking of a
child's leg in a fit of rage is likely to be more harmful to
the child than inappropriate sexual conduct of a minor
nature. We should be able and willing to extend basic social
work principles of respect and acceptance to these fathers
and a humanistic approach which, while reflecting the reality of their misconduct, is therapeutic in its nature and
intent.

The Fathers Anonymous Programme

As part of its beginning efforts to develop a comprehensive
family sexual misuse treatment programme3 and in response to
the treatment needs of fathers who have been sexually involved with their daughters, Oxford Family and Children's
Services has for the past year, operated a group treatment
programme for such fathers. The programme called Fathers
Anonymous, although still in its developmental phase has
achieved some modest success and may be of interest to practitioners providing treatment in the area of family sexual
misuse.

Treatment Principles
In addition to the generally accepted treatment principles
which underly all therapeutic activity, a number of specific
treatment principles are considered fundamental to the
Fathers Anonymous programme.

   1. The sexual abuse of children is unacceptable behaviour:
It is important to be clear and unequivocal in providing
treatment to fathers and their families that under no circumstances is the sexual abuse of children acceptable

behaviour. Amid society's changing values regarding sexual behaviour, one's own conflicting emotions, and the family's presentation of mitigating circumstances, it is essential to communicate, within the context of a willingness to assist, that the abuse is wrong, must stop and not be repeated.

2. Effective intervention should not destroy the family in the process: In this regard our endeavours are clearly humanistic and therapeutic in orientation. They are also geared to the rehabilitation of the family unit.

3. Sexual abuse of children is a family problem: Our programme is based on the conceptualization that father/daughter sexual misconduct is a manifestation of a dysfunctional family system. While we hold the father responsible at all times for his behaviour, we believe that the basic predisposing factors are found in faulty marriage and family relationships. Therefore, the whole family as well as the perpetrator require treatment involvement.

4. The meshing of the judicial system and the therapeutic system is essential for effective intervention: There is much discussion and unresolved debate respecting the involvement of the judicial system in a helping approach towards family sexual misconduct. Those opposing judicial involvement rightly stress the negative and impersonal impact of the legal system upon the whole family. Arrest, public trial with detailed evidence of intimate behaviour, daughters testifying against their fathers, incarceration, and loss of income are said to be more damaging to the child and family than the sexual misconduct itself. However, it is our experience that the involvement of the judicial system is helpful and at times essential for successful treatment. Firstly, it provides a means of expiation for the offender. Most of the men in our programme retroactively speak positively of this factor in their rehabilitation. Secondly, legal involvement provides a powerful, authoritative incentive for changing behaviour and stopping the abuse. In addition, we have found that once treatment alternatives have been established for family members and especially for the fathers, it is possible to influence a more humanistic approach by the legal system and to develop a more effective meshing of the judicial and helping systems. Finally, like it or not, the family sexual offences are going to remain within the Criminal Code for the foreseeable future. So, helping professions have to find effective ways to deal with the reality that the judicial system will continue to remain involved in these cases.

Treatment Goals
In our overall response to the treatment of family sexual
misuse we have identified specific treatment goals for each
of the participants and relationships involved. The treatment goals for the Fathers Anonymous programme are not an
end in themselves but rather should be seen within the content of this broader treatment approach.

1. To prevent further sexual misconduct.

2. To assist fathers in accepting responsibility for the
sexual misconduct: Here is it not sufficient for the father
to admit responsibility. He must also believe that this behaviour is wrong and must cease. Although the father may be
resistive to accepting responsibility or may feel guilty or
depressed, this issue must be firmly addressed and resolved.
The father's acceptance of full responsibility is the key to
restructuring of both the marriage relationship and family
relationships. Once the father has accurately assigned responsibility to himself, we expect him while in our programme
to acknowledge this to his wife and daughter and to apolog-
ize for his behaviour. All the men in our group have undertaken this activity. Although difficult for them this step
has proven to be a significant one for them in reducing
their self-loathing and in freeing them to undertake further
therapeutic activity.

3. To assist the fathers to understand the problem: It has
been our experience that most fathers do not comprehend how
or why the sexual misuse occurs. In our group sessions we
ask each father to examine and discuss the factors which led
up to the abuse. Specifically, we help them to:
- identify the stresses being experienced immediately
  prior to the abuse;
- identify their common response pattern in dealing with
  such stresses;
- explore the nature and quality of their marital relationship prior to and at the time of the sexual misuse;
- explore and identify the possible range of motives for
  their behaviour;
- explore what needs were not being fulfilled at the time
  of the misuse.

Where possible, we try to get the fathers in touch with
their feelings associated with the events, activities or
relationships they describe. Increased understanding of why
the misconduct occurred is helpful in clarifying for these
men what needs to be changed in their life and their relationships.

4. To enable fathers to assume expected roles as a spouse and parent: Many fathers have confused or inappropriate ideas as to their role as husband and father. In general, they exhibit dominant and narcisstic qualities. They have a reduced capacity for and ability to identify with the feeling states of others.

So, in our group sessions through experiential activities we try to assist these fathers in developing increased sensitivity to others. Here we focus on increasing their sensitivity to their children and spouse. In doing so, we address such issues as the effects of their sexual misconduct on each family member, and the use and misuse of power in the family. We also model and coach the fathers in developing communication patterns which are supportive and unambiguous.

Another area in which fathers need considerable help is to improve their capacity to give and receive appropriate affection. Many fathers report that their marriage relationship is emotionally and sexually unsatisfying. Here we use the group to get each father to identify and where necessary reduce their expectations from their marriage relationship in terms of emotional, affectional and intimacy needs. Once they have developed realistic expectations, we ask each father to initiate discussion with their spouses in order to understand their needs and to develop mutually accepted expectations.

Lastly, we try to assist fathers in defining appropriate behaviour in regard to their children. Here we try to identify clear role boundaries between child and parent. Specifically, we focus on what behaviour and responsibilities belong to parents and those which belong to children. For example, we establish what is appropriate and inappropriate physical affection between father and child. Here our intent is the establishment and maintenance of clear role boundaries and a clear direction to fathers that their needs for intimacy, affection and sex should be met within the marriage and not through their children.

Group Mechanics
Our Fathers Anonymous group meets weekly and is co-led by a male and female worker. We believe that joint leadership is helpful to the fathers. Firstly, they see a model of female/male partnership which is based on mutual respect and devoid of power plays. Secondly, the female leaders is helpful in providing them with insight and sensitivity to the female

perspective of sexual misconduct, marriage relationships and parenting. Thirdly, a female leader is essential for some of the role play activities undertaken in the group. To date we have experienced no negative effects from such a leadership arrangement.

Because we do not view all family sexual misuse as being similar or all offenders as having exactly the same characteristics, we do not view all fathers as treatable. Consequently, we have developed criteria for membership in our Fathers Anonymous group. This criteria includes:
- participants must be a father or father figure of some permanence;
- the absence of extended periods of treatment;
- the absence of extended periods of treatment and/or incarceration for similar behaviour or offences in the past;
- the absence of violent, sadistic or bizarre sexual behaviour such as rape or pornographic exploitation;
- the absence of substance abuse unless the father has terminated such usage and is engaged in an active treatment programme for this problem;
- suitable measures have been undertaken to ensure the protection of the daughter from further misuse;
- there is a common goal among husband, wife and children (including the daughter) to keep the family united or to reunite the family;
- there is a consensus on the part of the Court and the Agency that the offender/or family is viable and amenable to treatment;
- fathers who voluntarily admit responsibility for the misconduct or who are referred by court order are eligible to participate. A full admission is not a prerequisite in these latter cases.

All our group sessions are strictly confidential except in two circumstances. First, in the interest of further treatment where group members request or consent to a request for the release of specific information about themselves, we will provide the information. Second, in cases where members are court ordered to attend, we will provide on the request of the court or probation officer a summary of the group member's progress in the program. This report is shared with the group member and summarizes attendance, participation and involvement in the group, participant progress, and our recommendations. No specific details of the participant's disclosures or behaviour is provided in these reports. Court

ordered participants are accepting of this possible require-
ment and as long as it is effected through such a general
report which they have an opportunity to view. In practice,
we have not experienced any difficulty with respect to court
ordered participation in the program.

Some Modest Successes

It is still too early to evaluate the therapeutic effective-
ness of the Fathers Anonymous programme on any reliable
basis. However, we have ascertained some positive develop-
ments which we consider as indications of a modest success.
Firstly, the development and operation of the Fathers
Anonymous programme has been well accepted by the courts,
adult probation service and other members of the judicial
system. In some situations where a father has or intends to
plead guilty to a charge involving family sexual misconduct,
we have found the defence lawyer to be helpful in steering
the father into the programme. In other situations where a
father has been found guilty, the defence lawyer in speaking
to sentence may again argue for a term of probation with
mandatory attendance in our programme. The majority of participants in our programme have been court ordered. In
general, we are encouraged by this activity as we believe it
means for fathers the beginning of a more humanistic era
with respect to their treatment by the judicial system and
the possibility of a dispositional alternative to incarceration. Secondly, we have experienced perfect attendance and
active participation by all fathers in the programme. This
has enabled all the fathers to achieve some therapeutic
progress. In our judgment, significant gains have been made
in the area of fathers accepting the responsibility for
their behaviour. The group program has provided the first
real opportunity for these fathers to discuss openly and
fully their behaviour, their relationships and their feelings. In a supportive environment where they are held ac-
countable but not condemned most of the fathers have been
able to grow in self-esteem and to the point where they no
longer are disgusted by their own behaviour and are now able
to look outwards and initiate steps to restore their relationships with their wives and daugthers. Less progress has
been made in terms of increasing their level of empathy, and
their capacity to give and receive affection and emotional
support. While progress and change may be slow, it is en-

couraging that these men have the determination and potential to do so given the opportunity.

Notes

1. Louise Armstrong, *Kiss Daddy Goodnight*. New York:
   Pocket Books, 1978
2. Charlotte Vale Allen, *Daddy's Girl*. Toronto: McClelland
   & Stewart, 1980
3. This comprehensive approach includes individual and
   family therapy, group treatment for children, mother and
   father.

Reprinted with permission from *The Journal*, November 1982,
Vol 26, Ontario Association of Children's Aid Societies,
Toronto, Ontario, Canada.

# 8.  BETRAYAL OF TRUST: FATHER-DAUGHTER INCEST

CHERYL BOON

Abstract

In the spring of 1984 Cherly Boon prepared a paper on the
Long-Term Effects of Father-Daughter Incest, using the results of a survey of past victims she and two other researchers conducted at the University of Waterloo. Volunteer respondents were recruited through public notices in
southern Ontario and may provide a more unbiased representation of incest victims than studies of victims in therapy,
hospitals, or correctional institutions.
   The respondents who ranged in age from 18 to 72 years, had
stopped having sexual contact with their father or other
male caretaker an average of 20 years before completing the
questionnaires. On average, sexual abuse had begun at age
eight and ended at 13. Over 50 per cent reported that sexual
contact had occurred more than once a week; 46 per cent said
it had continued for five years or more. Intercourse
occurred in less than half the cases. Most victims said the
incest had serious long-term effects on their lives.

A growing body of evidence suggests that father-daughter incest often has serious long-term effects on the victim's
self-image, relationships with others and her sexuality.
   Incest is often experienced by the child as a violation of
trust by a respected parent on whom the child depends. The
experience is rarely, if ever, a loving, sensitive, or pleasurable one for the child.
   The guardian is almost always engaged in a selfish act for
his own pleasure – through dominance, power and sexual control. His actions are frequently rationalized by beliefs in
his 'property' rights as a male and as a parent, the failure
of his partner to meet sexual/emotional needs and his
attitude toward women.

Research has also shown that once the taboo on incest has
been broken, the victim is more vulnerable to being sexually
abused by other family members and by unrelated adults. Forty
per cent of women had had sexual contact with at least one
other family member and 30 per cent had sexual contact with
at least one other adult outside the family after the incest.

## Long-Term Effects

Our study found that only three of 77 women felt the incest
had had no effect on their lives. Effects reported by the
remainder were far-reaching and long-lasting.

Using standardized psychological tests, the victims showed
higher levels of distress and lower levels of social adjustment than community norms. Contrary to popular theory, there
was no evidence that these effects were related to the duration, frequency, or degree of sexual intimacy of the incest
experience.

Furthermore, there was no significant relationship between
these indicators and the age at which the incest had started
or stopped. These findings suggest that it is the incest itself, rather than other factors, which has the most bearing
on a survivor's adjustment.

The violation of trust by a parental figure also appeared
to have a deep and long-term effect on most incest survivors. This misturst may be made even more painful by disbe-
lieving or unhelpful responses when the victim talked about
her experience. The strong desire for love, intimacy, and
affirmation is often countered by a fear of becoming close,
vulnerable and misused.

One woman wrote: 'I feel hopeless in finding a man I can
relate to on equal terms and love fully without fear of him
taking advantage of me in a manner I don't want. I want to
love a man more than anything.'

But the common theme expressed by many women in these
questionnaires was the effects these early experiences had
on their sexuality. Many reported that they lost control
over their sexuality as a child and were left with the feeling that sex and sexuality was demeaning, shameful and re-
pugnant.

The fear of being caught and the silence to which she must
consent usually left a child feeling guilty and isolated
from peers, mother and siblings. Typically, she would begin
to feel 'dirty' and 'different.' In many cases, this loss of
control led to doubts about her ability to control other
important aspects of her life.

'Sexual Cripple'

Particularly disturbing was the finding that mistrust and
low self-esteem had made a deep impact on their sexuality.
Many of the women who participated in the study reported
problems feeling comfortable with sex and felt the incest
had made their sexual relationships difficult.

'I feel like a sexual cripple,' one woman wrote. Other
women pointed out specific effects on the way they respond-
ed sexually. 'I only get excited by violence and bondage
which really bothers me as I think of myself as a feminist
and hate violence against women,' another said. And from a
third: 'I have cut off my sexual feelings mostly.' Forty-
five per cent of the women reported at least some sexual
problems in their current relationships.

The women reported different patterns of relating to men
and to their sexuality. Some had decided that sexual and
intimate relationships were a confusing quagmire or too
threatening and felt unable to form close relationships with
others.

Other women reported that they had turned to women for
close sexual relations free from the underlying attitudes of
male sexuality. Many described patterns of successive brief
sexual encounters with men which were rooted in a desire to
be liked and/or difficulty turning men down.

Remain Sensitive

Many women were struggling to break their own perception
that the only way to obtain approval and affection with
others was through sex. The low self-esteem and underlying
mistrust experienced by many of these women can be a significant barrier in establishing satisfying intimate relationships.

From our research, we concluded that it was important for
counsellors, sex educators, health professionals and others
who deal with these women to remain sensitive and aware of
the nature and quality of these effects, especially in the
area of sexuality.

Reprinted with permission of *Tellus*, Winter 1984, Vol 5, No
4. Planned Parenthood Federation of Canada.

9. THE BADGLEY REPORT ON SEXUAL OFFENSES AGAINST CHILDREN

BENJAMIN SCHLESINGER

The Badgley Report on Sexual Offenses Against Children in
Canada (1984) contains two volumes of 1314 pages. It is the
most comprehensive study in Canada on three topics: Sexual
Abuse of Children, Juvenile Prostitution and Child Pornography. About three quarters of the report is devoted to
Sexual Abuse of Children. A committee of eleven persons met
for a period of three years to prepare the report (1981–
1984). Among the issues assigned to the Committee were:
- to document the extent of child sexual abuse and recommend how young victims can be better protected;
- to consider how juvenile prostitution could be prevented;
- to determine the extent of the making of child pornography and examine the accessibility of pornography to
  children.

The committee sponsored the following research related to
sexual abuse of Children (Table 1).

TABLE 1: Research Related to Sexual Abuse of Children

| Research Studies | Information Reviewed/Collected |
| --- | --- |
| 1. Legislative Reports/ Previous Research | Previous legislative/advisory reports; main Canadian research studies |
| 2. Legal Review | Legislative origins and subsequent amendments to major sexual offences; major legal decisions; legal status of the child; principles of evidence (evididence of children, corroboration, complaints by |

|  | victims, hearsay, previous sexual conduct, evidence of accused's spouse; similar acts; public access to hearings; publication of victims' names; proposed federal legislation; provincial child welfare statutes; legislation relating to prostitution and obscene materials. |
|---|---|
| 3. National Population Survey | 1008; Canadians in 210 communities, focussing on experience with having been sexually abused as children and youths, making of child pornography and assaults associated with exposure to pornography. |
| 4. National Police Force Survey | 6203 cases of sexually abused children; 28 police forces in 10 provinces and the Yukon. |
| 5. Child Protection Services | 1. Provincial child welfare statutes, including: child in need of proection; duty to report; and child abuse registers. 2. Special community services. 3. 1438 cases of sexually abused children: National Child Protection Survey, 10 provinces and the Yukon. |
| 6. Health Services | 1. 612 sexually abused children: National Hospital Survey, 11 hospitals in 8 provinces. 2. Genetic risks of incest: major research studies reviewed. 3. Sexually Transmitted Diseases: treatment and risks relative to 452 children having these conditions. 4. Criminal Injuries Compensation Boards – review of cases given compensation. |

| 7. Publicity | 1. 2806 stories concerning sexual offence cases in 34 Canadian newspapers. 2. Legal reporting services listing court decisions and reported judicial decisions, between 1970–82. |
| --- | --- |
| 8. Historical Crime Statistics | From 1876–1973, rates of charges laid; types and lengths of sentences; conviction rates. |
| 9. Convicted Child Sexual Offenders | 703 convicted child sexual offenders: National Corrections Survey – 10 correctional services (federal and provincial. |
| 10. Child Sexual Assault Homicides | 156 child sexual assault homicides, 1961–80. |
| 11. Dangerous Child Sexual Offenders | 62 offenders found by courts to be dangerous in relation to sexual offences against children; full listing of all such offenders. |

In total there were 10,272 cases of sexual abuse examined.

From its research, the Committee found that:
- At some time during their lives, about one in two females and one in three males have been victims of one or more unwanted sexual acts. These acts include: being exposed to; being sexually threatened; being touched on a sexual part of the body; and attempts to assault or being sexually assaulted.
- About four in five of these unwanted sexual acts had been first committed against these persons when they were children or youths.
- Four in 100 of young females have been raped.
- Two in 100 of young persons have experienced attempts or actual acts of unwanted anal penetration by a penis, or by means of objects or fingers.
- Acts of exposure constituted the largest single category of sexual offences committed against children. Cases were documented where such acts were followed by sexual assault.
- Three in five sexually abused children had been threatened or physically coerced by their assailants. Young victims are as likely to be threatened or forced to

   engage in sexual acts by persons relatively close in age
   as by older persons.
   - Few young victims were physically injured; substantially
     more suffered emotional harms.
   - About one in four assailants is a family member or a
     person in a position of trust; about half are friends or
     acquaintances; and about one in six is a stranger.
   - Virtually all assailants are males; one in 100 is a fe-
     male.
   - A majority of victims or their families do not seek as-
     sistance from public services. When they do, they turn
     most often to the police and doctors.
   - Over two in five of all sexual assault homicides are
     commited against children age 15 and younger. Children
     are victims of three in four convicted sexual offenders
     found to be dangerous on sentencing by courts.
The research also shows, that of sexually abused children
serviced by child protection workers:
   - Half of the initial assessments were undertaken within
     48 hours of notification; two-thirds were completed
     within a week.
   - Half of these children were reported to have been med-
     ically examined.
   - Beyond contacts with the police and doctors, other help-
     ing services were contacted in only a small proportion
     of cases.
   - Interviews by workers were held, on average, with: three
     in four victims; seven in 10 mothers; less than half of
     the fathers; less than half of the suspected offenders;
     about two in five of the child's brothers or sisters.
   - Children who had been victims of serious sexual acts
     were as likely to be left in their homes as to have been
     removed. There was no relationship between the removal
     of offenders and the various types of sexual acts com-
     mitted.
   Some other findings of the research included the follow-
ing:

Statistics
On the basis of its review, the Committee concluded that
existing official statistical reporting systems (police,
homicides, corrections, disease classification, child protection services) are virtually worthless in serving to
identify the reported occurrence and circumstances of child
sexual abuse. Without exception, all of these statistical

reporting systems are so seriously flawed that they do not
provide even rudimentary information about the victims of
sexual offences, whether they are children, youths or
adults.

There are no provincial or national statistics of how many
sexual offences against children have been investigated by
the police. Accurate statistics in this regard are virtually
non-existent among child protection services. The system of
medical classification of injuries fails to identify the
major types of sexual assaults committed against victims.
The available statistics on sentencing do not permit judges
to be able to assess the efficacy of their decisions imposed
upon convicted child sexual offenders. Official reporting
systems also contain significant omissions about those offenders who are deemed to be among the most dangerous crim-
inals in the country, many of whom have been convicted of
sexual offences against children.

In light of these deficiencies, it is hardly surprising
that at the present time we have a very imperfect understanding of the officially reported occurrence of sexual
offences against children. Given even the lowest estimates
of the extent of child sexual abuse in Canada, the problem
is a matter of grave public concern. Until more reliable and
comprehensive information is available on a continuing
basis, it will remain a matter of conjecture how many
Canadian children who are sexually assaulted are known to
and served by public agencies.

Child Abuse Registers
Registers (or analogous record-keeping systems) are author-
ized by the child welfare legislation of eight provinces. On
the basis of its research, the Committee found that:
  - A sizeable proportion of cases of child sexual abuse
    known to the police, physicians and child protection
    workers was not reported to child abuse registers.
  - Proportionately more minor than serious sexual offences
    were reported.
  - Child protection workers had consulted registers in re-
    lation to only one in five cases which were open.
  - Several provinces having registers had no formal pro-
    cedures with respect to the periodic review of cases
    listed in the files of registers.
In relation to the reporting of child sexual abuse,
provincial child abuse registers are clearly not being used
to the extent or in the manner intended by legislators. The

utility of their functions appears also to be severly limited as case catalogues, research aids or assessment tools.

Services
Each of the main helping services has developed somewhat
different concepts of child protection, different means for
assessing and investigating the needs of young victims, different standards in determining how assistance can best be
provided and different ways of providing such help. Our research indicates that, as a result of these different perspectives, many sexually abused children either received no
assessment or their needs were only partially and inade-
quately considered. Because of insufficient follow-up, many
were left in situations of continuing risk.
    To redress these deficiencies, the Committee believes that
a combination of measures is required, including: publicizing widely the work of special programmes; the adoption of
common mimimum standards between services for the assessment, investigation and treatment of sexually abused children; introducing significant changes in provincial child
welfare legislation and the current operation of the child
abuse registers; and the development of medical examination
protocols.
    The committee made 52 recommendations, one of the main
ones was the establishment of an 'Office of a Commissioner.'
(Summary , 1984, 13-14)

    For the reasons given, we believe that the Government of
    Canada should establish an Office of the Commissioner,
    reporting directly to the Office of the Prime Minister,
    having the assigned authority to review the recommenda-
    tions of this Report and serving as the means of initiat-
    ing and co-ordinating the reforms which are called for.
    Assigned its own budgetary allocation for these purposes,
    the Office of the Commissioner would initiate and co-
    ordinate the work of various federal departments at the
    provincial level and establish the means needed to assure
    the full participation of non-governmental agencies in
    these activities.
    Where special needs have been recognized in the past
    (Human Rights, Status of Women), the Government of Canada
    has established special bodies which are assigned respon-
    sibility to respond to these issues. On the basis of our
    findings, there can be no doubt that the establishment of
    an Office of the Commissioner is warranted in order to

initiate and marshall the efforts of all levels of government and non-governmental agencies, having as their common
purpose, the provision of services required to reduce and
prevent child sexual abuse.

## Implications for Child Protection Agencies

The Committee believes that child protection workers are
hampered in their efforts to help sexually abused children.
The referral process provided for in child protection legislation does not specify clearly whether child sexual abuse
cases are to be dealt with under child protection legislation or under the provisions of the federal Criminal Code.
Police, hospital and agency officials do not, therefore, always refer cases to child protection workers. Of cases referred, one-third take over a week to reach child workers.
Of those handled, interviews take place with three out of
four victims, seven out of ten mothers, less than half of
the fathers, less than half of the suspected offenders and
two out of five siblings.

Two intervention strategies are suggested. The first is a
child-centred approach combining interdisciplinary team-
work, a victim orientation and the use of child protection
staff trained in sexual abuse procedures. The second, a
family-centred approach, emphasizes multidisciplinary consultation, family orientation and the use of general child
protection staff. It is a voluntary form of intervention
which assumes thaht the criminal justice system be used as a
last resort.

## Implications for Health Services

A lack of national standards results in insufficient assessment for children who have been sexually abused. Children
are left in situations where abuse may continue and the risk
of venereal disease is high. The Committee's recommendations
to remedy the situation include adoption of common minimum
national standards, the development of medical examination
procedures, the operation of child abuse registers and increased publicizing of the work of special programs.

## Legal Implications

Existing civil and criminal laws dealing with childhood
sexual abuse lack a central purpose and rationale. The

Committee proposes that there be a clarification of unacceptable behaviours including sexual intercourse with young
girls, incest, buggery, bestiality, genital and anal acts
involving children, abuse of positions of trust and acts of
genital exposure. In general, the Committee concludes that
where the wording for several offences is vague, charges can
be laid for the same behaviour under different sections of
the Criminal Code, each having different maximum penalties.
   In the existing system of penalties, the length of the
sentence does not necessarily match the seriousness of the
offence. Even where similar types of sexual acts have been
committed, the average lengths of the sentences vary sharply.

Implications for Police Services

The Committee found that police regard victims of sexual
abuse under the age of 12 as more credible than those victims between 16 and 20 years of age. Police accept that 9
out of 10 reported cases are valid. The decision of police
to proceed in a case is influenced by the types of sexual
offences and the sex and age of the victim. For instance,
where a victim is under seven years, police will generally
not lay a charge because no court will accept the testimony
of young children without corroborating evidence or the
testimony of an adult. If a social agency intervenes on behalf of the child, the police will not lay charges. The
Committee recommends improved co-ordination and co-operation
among police, social workers and legal professionals.

Further Research Needed

Childhood sexual abuse requires intervention by a variety of
disciplines. However, research to date has represented the
work of single disciplines and has therefore led to a frag-
mented approach to the problem. Furthermore studies have
failed to provide a sufficient foundation upon which to base
law reform or to restructure services. The Committee suggests the establishment of the Office of a Commissioner, reporting directly to the Prime Minister, with a mandate to
co-ordinate the sharing of information and to oversee funding for new research.

Conclusion

The summary of the report points out that child sexual abuse
is a largely hidden yet pervasive tragedy that has damaged

the lives of tens of thousands of Canadian children and youths. For most of them, their needs remain unexpressed and unmet. These silent victims – and there are substantial numbers of them – are often those in greatest need of care and help. Only a few young victims of sexual offences seek assistance from the helping services and there are sharp disparities in the types and adequacy of the services provided for them in different parts of the country.

What is now lacking is any widely agreed upon policy providing for an orderly, comprehensive and rational development and provision of services for the assistance and care of sexually abused children. The obstacles that now hinder the achievement of better protection for sexually abused children are not insurmountable. While in the short run they represent serious barriers to realizing this aim, many of these problems can be resolved by an energetic and joint endeavour involving all levels of government working in full co-operation with non-governmental organizations.

Canadians are deeply concerned about the need to provide better protection for sexually abused and exploited children and youths. This strongly held concern is national in scope. It cuts across all social, religious and political boundaries. It encompasses all forms of sexual abuse of the child, whether this involves sexual assault, juvenile prostitution or the making of child pornography.

Note: The recommendations can be found in the two-volume report and in the summary.

References

Badgley, R.F., *Sexual Offenses Against Children*. Ottawa: Canadian Government Publishing Centre, 1984, 2 vols ($25.00)
Canadian Government Publishing Centre, *Sexual Offenses Against Children: Summary*. Ottawa: 1984 ($3.95)

## 10.  SEXUAL ABUSE OF CHILDREN: A NATIONAL HYSTERIA?

SOL GORDON

Children need to be hugged, kissed and cuddled more, not less. Of course, sexual abuse is a serious problem. The appropriate response, though, is not hysteria. What is required is a national programme of sexuality education beginning with askable parents who respond to the natural curiosity of their children at ages 2, 3 or 4. (If a parent has a shy child who doesn't ask, it's up to the parent to initiate a discussion before the age of 5.)

The parent also must be prepared to use the correct terminology. What's all this nonsense about 'private parts?' It's all right to use this collective term, but not without explaining to what the term refers: penis, vulva, vagina, breast or anus. It is now entirely legitimate and desirable to use the correct terminology. (I actually said these words on 'Good Morning America' on 1 February 1985 – an historic moment in America's Sexual Revolution.)

No, we don't have to frighten children in order to safeguard them. Children who are loved, appreciated, listened to, believed, sexually educated and *prepared* for the possibility of bad things happening have the best *possible* protection they can get.

But alas, this is not an entirely safe world for children. Children need to be sensibly prepared – not by telling them (without explanation) that there is bad and good touching (sexual and seductive touching often feels good). Right and wrong touching is a better approach. In addition, let's not create an illusion that all a child has to do is say, 'No.' An abuser who knows the child well (which is true in about 75% of the cases) can take advantage of a child whether the child likes it or not. Children can be prepared by conveying to them that 'If you are forced to do bad things, it's okay to lie and promise you won't tell. Then, when you get away, tell someone you trust.'

We educators had better warn parents not to get hysterical. Many adults, who as children reported sexual abuse to their parents, have revealed that they were either not believed or punished, or that the overreaction of their parents seemed to them worse than the abuse itself. Professionals who are told about abuse had better help develop a support system for the child lest the 'reporting' results in even more abuse for the child in the courts and social service system.

No, you don't have to worry if children are warned about sexual touching that they will grow up sexually dysfunctional. Children who are touched, loved, and caressed by parents and relatives who care about them have a better chance of making the transition to mature adult sexual behaviour.

And enough hysteria about letting children visit with grandparents or being hugged by nursery school teachers. A lot of commonsense combined with a *little* extra precaution about choosing and being able to visit a nursery school or camp at any time is sufficient. The risks of children being hurt are not so great that we must deprive them of the experience of being with relatives, teachers or friends. The basic security of the child, including the speed of recovery when something bad does happen, must rest with the parents. There is no other way.

Surely, we must tell children about strangers, but children can still be friendly to *anyone* when accompanied by parents, and children can be encouraged to respond appropriately to teachers in school.

For heaven's sake, let's not overreact to a 13- or 14-year-old who, due to his or her unresolved and uneducated impulses, engages in exploratory play with children of a younger age. But coercive sexual behaviour warrants attention. Teenagers' 'experiments' with much younger children must always be designated as coercive. However, the teenagers need treatment, not a prison. But here, too, we have to evaluate the difference between single experiences and chronic behaviour.

One final plea to all you folks in the sexual abuse/abduction field: Please include sex educators and child development specialists as part of the mission. If you did, enduring impairment and trauma to children would be effectively decreased. You would lose fewer cases in the legal justice system and, hopefully, you would be less concerned about the 'moral majority' not liking you if you allow sexuality to be included in your deliberations about sexual abuse. You will also investigate all abuse accusations more carefully before you move to legal action.

Sex educators and child psychologists know very well that no one theory about abuse fits all cases. We know that the dynamics of the pedophile are probably different from those of people who are involved in incest. But there are *some* generalizations that can be made: Very few abusers have had an adequate sex education and very few have a healthy attitude about masturbation. It also would be hard to find a single sexual abuser or pedophile who has had a healthy, mature relationship with an adult girlfriend or wife. At this time, so little is known about women abusers that generalizations about their behaviour and dynamics cannot be made.

We need sanity in this area. We need to work together. Include sex educators and child development specialists as part of your team. The field is not complete without us.

Reprinted with permission of the author and *Impact '85*, 1985. Institute for Family Research and Education, Syracuse, N.Y., U.S.A.

ANNOTATED BIBLIOGRAPHY

Abuse of Boys

1. Ellerstein, N.S. and J.W. Canavan. 'Sexual Abuse of
   Boys,' *American Journal of Diseases of Children*, 134
   (March 1980) 255-7
   A retrospective review of 145 sexually abused children
   of whom 11 per cent were male. The boys were more
   likely to be assaulted in a public place than were the
   girls.

2. Nasjleti, M. 'Suffering in Silence: The Male Incest
   Victim,' *Child Welfare*, 59 (May 1980) 269-75
   Male incest victims have been virtually ignored by
   most investigators of incest, and little information
   about them is available in the literature. Large gaps
   still exist in the social worker's understanding of the
   dyanamics of child sexual abuse.
   Since fewer male than female victims of incest come
   to the attention of law enformcement agencies, most
   social workers in public agencies have limited knowledge of and experience with male victims. The study of
   male incest victims is long overdue. This paper fills
   part of this gap by examining reasons boys remain
   silent victims of incest.
   The author's involvement in the Sacramento Child
   Sexual Abuse Treatment Program has included initiating
   and co-leading a group therapy experience for adolescent male incest victims. The co-leader is a male
   social worker whose professional training and work
   are similar to the author's.

3. Nielsen, T. 'Sexual abuse of boys: current perspectives.' *Personnel and Guidance Journal*, 62 (Nov. 1983)
139–42
The purpose of this article is to compile information
from the most recent literature concerning the sexual
abuse of boys; a rather unique clinical group whose
needs have not been dealt with adequately. Included in
the discussion are dynamics, prevalence, reluctance to
report, nature of the offenders, and subsequent
implications in counseling. While boys are more
frequently sexually exploited by a non-family member
than are girls, a stranger is not likely to be the
offender; assaults on children by strangers represent
only a slight percentage of child sexual abuse, and
tend to be single episodes in contrast to victimization
by family members or acquaintances, which is more
likely to take place over and over for a period of
time. The perpetrator is far more likely to be someone
who has developed a close relationship with the child,
someone the child probably trusts, and someone he or
she cares for. The number of boys involved in reported
sexual abuse has risen considerably in recent years;
professionals indicate that boys now comprise 25 to 35
per cent of their case loads.

4. Sarrel, P.M. and W.H. Masters. 'Sexual Molestation of
Men by Women,' *Archives of Sexual Behavior*, 11:2, 1982,
117–31
The belief that it is impossible for males to respond
sexually when subjected to sexual molestation by women
is contradicted. Previous research indicating that
male sex response can occur in a variety of emotional
states, including anger and terror, are corroborated.
Eleven cases of male sexual molestation by females are
classified and described.  A post-trauma reaction
occurs in which sexual function and psychological state
are affected. The men were all personally interviewed.
Recognition of this phenomenon should lead to increased
identification of male victims as well as to better
medical, psychological, and legal services for them.

Adolescents and Sexual Abuse

5. Ageton, S.S. *Sexual Assault among Adolescents.*
Lexington, Mass.: Lexington Books, 1984

This book approaches the field of adolescent sexual
assault, and draws upon data from a five-year study to
present estimates of its national incidence and prevalence. It offers a detailed demographic, attitudinal,
and behavioral profile of both adolescent victims and
offenders, discusses the initial impact and long-term
effects of being sexually victimized, and focuses on
personal characteristics, environmental conditions,
attitudinal sets, and behavioral indices which seem to
be predictive of an adolescent's becoming a sexual-
assault victim or offender.

6. Anderson, L.S. 'Notes on the Linkage between the
   Sexually Abused Child and the Suicidal Adolescent,'
   *Journal of Adolescence*, 4 (June 1981) 157-62
   Case material is used to illustrate how sexual abuse
   during childhood can result in later self-
   destructiveness. Many sexually abused children are
   vulnerable to feelings of guilt, depression, and
   unworthiness that are exacerbated once they reach
   adolescence and have to deal with their own sexual
   development. Motivating factors in suicide attempts,
   treatment approaches, and the goals of therapy are
   discussed. The occurrence of sexual abuse is documented, and ways of recognizing the symptoms of sexual
   abuse are outlined.

7. Knittle, B.J. and S.J. Tuana. 'Group Therapy as Primary
   Treatment for Adolescent Victims of Intrafamilial
   Sexual Abuse,' *Clinical Social Work Journal*, 8 (4)
   1980, 236-42
   This article describes the therapeutic needs of adolescent victims of sexual abuse and presents the case
   that group therapy more effectively addresses these
   needs than individual or family therapies.

8. Shamroy, J.A. 'A Perspective on Childhood Sexual
   Abuse,' *Social Work*, 25 (March 1980) 128-31
   In 1977, the Cincinnati Children's Hospital treated 78
   pre-adolescent children for symptoms, signs or complaints of sexual abuse. The alleged abuser was known
   to the children in 72 per cent of the cases. This article describes the hospital's procedure for identifying these children and the follow-up services necessary
   for their protection and emotional adjustment.

9. Wayne, J. and K.K. Weeks. 'Groupwork with Abused
   Adolescent Girls: A Special Challenge,' *Social Work
   with Groups*, 7 (Winter 1984) 83-104
   Youthful victims of abuse and neglect can be helped to
   cope with their situations through group treatment.
   Their often provocative behaviour, however, makes them
   especially difficult to work with. The paper focuses
   on both therapeutic techniques with this population and
   ways to help the workers deal with the personal stress
   created by working with acting-out group members.

## Bibliographies on Sexual Abuse

10. Bagley, C. *Child Sexual Abuse within the Family: An
    Account of Studies 1978-1984.* Calgary: Faculty of
    Social Welfare, University of Calgary, 1985. (2500
    University Dr, N.W., Calgary, Alta. T2N 1N4)
    A comprehensive annotated bibliography dealing with
    sexual abuse of children. Films and visual materials
    are also included.

11. Carlsson, B. *Sexual Use of Children: A Bibliography.*
    Osterkar, Sweden: 1984. (Osterkarsvagen 11, S-184 02
    Osterkar, Sweden)
    The data in this bibliography has been obtained from
    national searches, visits to different countries and
    through individuals, organizations and universities.
    The information contained is not complete, and some of
    the older material has been left out. The bibliography
    deals with sexual use of children and has not been
    limited to sexual exploitation, firstly because there
    is a need for a bibliography that covers the whole
    field and secondly because it is difficult to draw a
    strict line between different forms of sexual use of
    children. The connections between the different forms
    are many and important.

12. Carrière, R. and A. Thomson. *Family Violence: A
    Bibliography of Ontario Resources, 1980-1984.* Sudbury,
    Ont.: Laurentian University, 1985
    This comprehensive bibliography attempts to record all
    work in the province of Ontario, related to family
    violence, including sexual abuse during the 1980-84
    period.

13. Clearinghouse on Child Abuse and Neglect Information. Bibliographies on varied topics related to sexual abuse. Washington, D.C., 1982–84 (P.O. Box 1182, Washington, D.C., 20013)

14. Dabney, M.L.F. *Incest: Annotated Bibliography.* Eugene, Or.: Melodye L.F. Dabney, 1983 (2000 Hawkins Lane, Eugene, Or., 97405)
    This self-published, first edition bibliography sites over 300 sources covering theoretical perspectives from the fields of psychology, education, counselling, medicine, law enforcement, and sociology. Resources are current through 1982.

15. Meredith, C. *Overview and Annotated Bibliography of Needs of Crime Victims.* Ottawa, Ont.: Ministry of the Solicitor General, 1984
    An annotated bibliography including sexual abuse and incest.

16. Ministry of the Solicitor General. *Child Abuse: A Bibliography.* Ottawa, Ont.: National Victims Resource Ctr, 1984 (340 Laurier Ave. W., Ottawa, Ont. K1A OP8)
    A non-annotated bibliography which includes child molesting and incest.

17. Rubin, R. and G. Byerly. *Incest, The Last Taboo: An Annotated Bibliography.* New York, N.Y.: Garland, 1983
    This book is a selective, annotated bibliography on incest encompassing psychological, sociological, anthropological, medical, scientific, legal, popular, and literary perspectives. Limited to works primarily concerned with the occurrence or discussion of incest in contemporary American society, the book includes monographs, dissertations, journal articles, and audiovisual materials published or produced in English. Chapters on incest from books of a broader scope are typically not included. Emphasis is on works published in the last ten years although significant monographs, dissertations, and articles published in the 1960s and before have been included.

18. Speert-Lawton, S. and A. Wachtel. *Child Sexual Abuse and Incest: An Annotated Bibliography.* Vancouver,

B.C.: United Way of the Lower Mainland, 1982, 2nd ed.
An annotated bibliography of 68 items up to 1981.

19. Tamarack, L.I. and I. Mountain. *A Bibliography on
Incest and Related Topics: Our Story of Survival*.
Ottawa, Ont.: The Healing Centre for Women, 1984
(P.O. Box 4861, Stn. F, Ottawa, Ont. K1S 5J1)
A mimeographed 27 page bibliography (not annotated) and
an introduction related to incest, rape, and prostitu-
tion.

20. U.S. Dept. of Health and Human Services. *Child Abuse
and Neglect Thesaurus*. Washington, D.C.: Clearinghouse
on Child Abuse and Neglect Information, 1983 (P.O. Box
1182, Washington, D.C., 20013)
The *Child Abuse and Neglect Thesaurus* is a compilation
of standardized words and phrases that are used to
characterize and describe child abuse and neglect information. As such, it serves several purposes:
- it lists contemporary terminology in the field
- it serves as a dictionary with authoritative spell-
  ings and prescribed usages
- it resolves questions of synonymous terms
- it specifies consistency in the use of word forms
- it displays generic and hierarchical relationship
  among terms
The *Thesaurus* was developed for use in operating the
information clearinghouse of the National Center on
Child Abuse and Neglect. It is used as the source of
terminology for the subject indexes that appear in
*Child Abuse and Neglect Research: Projects and Publica-
tions*, *Child Abuse and Neglect Programs*, and *Child
Abuse and Neglect Audiovisual Materials*. The *Thesaurus*
also is the source of descriptors for indexing the
documents, research summaries, programme descriptions,
and audiovisual materials in the computer-based NCCAN
data base. Because it is used for indexing, the
*Thesaurus* provides an authoritative list of suitable
search terms and their synonyms, and it helps a search-
er expand or restrict a search according to the subject
being sought. The subject terms in the *Thesaurus* are
used by the clearinghouse to search the data base in
response to queries received from organizations and individuals seeking information on child abuse and
neglect. Persons outside of the National Center who

have access to NCCAN data base will also find the
*Theasaurus* useful in formulating search strategies.

21. Valade, R., Lips, T. and F. Mes. 'Bibliography on Child
Abuse,' *Canada's Mental Health*, 32 (June 1984) B1-B8
A comprehensive bibliography on child abuse, including
items on sexual abuse (not annotated).

## Case Studies

22. Cooper, I. and B.M. Cormier. 'Inter Generational Transmission of Incest,' *Canadian Journal of Psychiatry*, 27
(April 1982) 231-5
It is possible for incest to involve three generations
and be 'transmitted' from one generation to the next
through several patterns. The psychodynamics of these
patterns of intergenerational transmission of incest
are described, with clinical examples from the author's
work and the literature.

23. Goodwin, J.M. 'Suicide Attempts in Sexual Abuse Victims
and their Mothers,' *Child Abuse and Neglect*, 5 (3)
1981, 217-22
A study on the frequency of suicide attempts in families where sexual abuse had been substantiated is reported. Records of a protective service agency were
reviewed for suicide attempts that occurred during the
36-month study period. Two hundred and one cases were
substantiated during this period.

24. MacFarlane, K. and J. Korbin. 'Confronting the Incest
Secret Long after the Fact: A Family Study of Multiple
Victimization with Strategies for Intervention.' *Child
Abuse & Neglect*. 7 (2) 1983, 225-37
Describes the case history of an extended family in
which all 11 adult females in one generation had experienced childhood sexual abuse by either a father/
uncle or an older cousin/brother. The sexual abuse had
been a closely guarded secret of each victim for up to
20 years despite the fact that all of the sisters had
close and frequent involvement in one another's lives.
Protection of the young daughter of the cousin/brother
provided the impetus for disclosure and a focal point
of concern for the SS whose sexual abuse had been
initiated at approximately the same age as the girl.

25. Rimsza, M.E. and E.H. Niggemann. 'Medical Evaluation of
    Sexually Abused Children: A Review of 311 Cases,'
    *Pediatrics*, 69 (January 1982) 8–14
    The case records of 311 children and adolescents who
    were medically evaluated for sexual abuse are review-
    ed. Only 18 per cent of these victims were assaulted by
    strangers: 131 of the assailants were relatives. Thirty
    per cent of the victims reported multiple assaults over
    a period of one week to nine years. Physical examina-
    tion showed no abnormalities in only 23 per cent of the
    patients. Twenty-one patients had gonorrhea and seven
    patients were pregnant.  Guidelines for the medical
    evaluation of patients suspected to be victims of
    sexual abuse are discussed.

26. Wells, L.A. 'Family Pathology and Father-daughter
    Incest: Restricted Psychopathy,' *Journal of Clinical
    Psychiatry*, 42 (May 1981) 197–202
    Presents three cases of father-daughter incest, each of
    which illustrates a primary pattern of dysfunction:
    sociopathy, restricted psychopathy, and family chaos.
    A family perspective is used that also considered the
    role of the siblings, mother and grandparents. Treat-
    ment considerations and the ramifictions of restricted
    psychopathy are discussed.

Childrens' Books

27. Adams, C.P. and J. Fay. *No More Secrets: Protecting
    Your Child from Sexual Assault*. San Luis Obispo,
    Calif.: Impact Publishers, 1981 (P.O. Box 1094, San
    Luis Obispo, Calif., 93406)
    Most parents assume that any sexual assault on a child
    will come from a weird stranger, will involve violence
    or coercion, and be an isolated, extreme incident. The
    opposite is true: 85 per cent of the time the assault
    is by someone the child knows, involves bribery and
    threats rather than extreme physical force, develops
    gradually over a period of time, and involves frequent
    incidents taking many forms.
       This illustrated paperback gives much useful advice
    on how to prepare children to say 'No' to sexually as-
    saultive acquaintances and seek the immediate help of
    their parents.

28. Colao, F. and T. Hosansky. *Your Children Should Know*.
    New York, N.Y.: Berkley Books, 1985
    A book which discusses what children should know in
    protecting themselves from sexual assault.

29. Citizens Concerned with Crime against Children.
    *Talking and Drawing about It*. Kitchener, Ont.: 1984
    (P.O. Box 1715, Stn C, Kitchener, Ont. N2G 4R3
    This is a colouring book for kids aged five years and
    up. It is designed to show victims and would-be vic-
    tims that they can overcome or even avoid the trauma of
    sexual abuse.
    - by talking about it with adults whom they trust, and
    - by learning the vital distinctions between 'good
      touching' and 'bad touching' - and that, in the
      latter case, they often have the option of saying
      'NO!' and that that choice is the RIGHT choice.

30. Dayee, F.S. *Private Zone: A Book Teaching Children
    Sexual Assault Prevention Tools*. Edmonds, Wash.:
    Charles Franklin Press, 1985 (90th Ave. W., Edmunds,
    WA, 98020)
    The book is designed to make children aware that access
    to certain parts of their bodies belongs to them and
    them alone. As such, the book uses simple language and
    constant repetition coupled with reasonable explana-
    tions to facilitate the imprinting of its message on a
    young mind.
       The concept of private zones is illustrated in such a
    way that most children should be able to understand.
    The book also makes very clear just who can touch your
    private zone and when. Above all, it emphasizes how im-
    portant each individual is.

31. Gordon, S. and J. Gordon. *A Better Safe than Sorry
    Book: A Family Guide for Sexual Assault Prevention*.
    Syracuse, N.Y.: Ed-U Press, 1984 (P.O. Box 583,
    Fayetteville, N.Y., 13066)
    The task of this book is to teach three to nine-year-
    olds about sexual assault.

32. Independent Order of Foresters. *What Everyone Should
    Know About the Sexual Abuse of Children*. Don Mills,
    Ont.: 1981

This illustrated booklet, geared to children discusses child sexual abuse.

33. Lenett, R. with B. Crane. *It's OK to Say No!* New York, N.Y.: Tor Books, 1985 (8-10 West 36th St., New York, N.Y. 10016)
This book is a read-aloud together book designed to help parents teach their children the rules of body-safety – what their kids need to know to avoid being victims of attempted sexual abuse or abduction. Each of the thirty brief stories in the book specifically illustrates how a potentially dangerous situation for a child might arise and how that crisis might then be handled by the youngster. The aim of the stories is to help children develop, through playacting and direct interactive communication with parents, an awareness of their rights when dealing with adults, whether those adults are strangers or well known to the child. While the stories are intended for children between the ages of three and ten, the guidelines in the first section of the book provide advice that will be useful in opening up communications with pre-teens and teenagers as well.

34. Longo, R.E. *The Prevention of Child Sexual Abuse.* Gainesville, Fla.: Health and Rehabilitation Services, 1982 (3rd Fl., 2002 NW 13th St., Gainesville, Fla. 32601)
In this booklet the author dispels the myths about child sexual assault, and instructs the reader on how to talk to children about sexual abuse.

35. Sweet, P.E. *Something Happened to Me.* Racine, Wis.: Mother Courage Press, 1983 (1533 Illinois St., Racine, Wis. 53405)
This short book with its drawings of children and simple text, could assist almost any child who has been sexually molested. It would interest parents or foster parents dealing with such a child, or a social worker or therapist doing ongoing treatment with a child.

36. Wachter, O. *No More Secrets for Me.* Toronto, Ont.: Little Brown and Co., 1984
A sensitive message for children as a weapon against child sexual abuse.

37. Williams, J. *Red Flag, Green Flag People*. Fargo, N.
    Dakota: Rape and Abuse Crisis Centre, 1980 (P.O. Box
    1655, Fargo, N.D. 58107)
    This is a colouring book for children to help them
    become aware of the dangers of sexual assault and in-
    cest. The book identifies different kinds of touch and
    shows children what to do when they are touched in an
    inappropriate manner.

38. Williams, J. *Once I was a Little Bit Frightened*.
    Fargo, N. Dakota: Rape and Crisis Centre, 1980
    Designed to be read to children in grades kindergarten
    through fifth, this book helps professionals and
    teachers determine if a child is a victim of sexual
    abuse and encourages the child to seek help.

## Conference Proceedings

39. Barnard, C.P. (ed.) *Families, Incest, and Therapy*. New
    York: N.Y.: Human Sciences Press, 1984
    Growing out of a conference designed to 'provide an
    understanding of incest and suggestions for interven-
    tion within a family context,' this special issue of
    *the International Journal of Family Therapy* provides
    the reader with a blend of theory, pragmatic treatment
    considerations, and illustrative clinical vignettes.
    Regarding incest as a complex clinical issue, the mate-
    rial contained in this volume provides greater clarity
    of understanding and ideas for clinical implementation.
    The reader, whether novice or experienced clinician,
    will find the contents a valuable source of information
    regarding incestuous families.

40. *Childhood and Sexuality: Proceedings of the Inter-
    national Symposium 1979*. Saint Laurent, Que.: Editions
    Etudes Vivantes, 1980
    This publication is not strictly directed to special-
    ists in sexology but is of interest to persons seeking
    information concerning children and their sexuality:
    educators, psychologists, social workers, specialists
    in learning disabilities, criminologists...
    Keeping with the spirit of the International Year of
    the Child, the Department of Sexology of the
    Université du Québec à Montréal, and the Association
    des Sexologues du Québec organized an international

symposium entitled 'Childhood and Sexuality.' Held at
the Université à Montréal, on the 7th, 8th, and 9th of
September 1979, this symposium quickly became a great
success, as over seventy research papers were presented
before a large audience.
 For many people, even for professionals, this symposium revealed the importance of the child's sexual life.
 Part seven contains 12 papers in English and French
related to Child Sexual Abuse.

41. Kemp, J.A. and D. Williams, eds. *Sexual Abuse of
Children Conference*. Winnipeg, Man.: Dept of the
Attorney General, 1982
Sixteen papers are presented on various aspects of
sexual abuse of children.

Education and Sexual Abuse

42. Bloom, E.V. 'Teacher Will You Listen?' *The British
Columbia Teacher*, Nov-Dec 1982, 68-72
Sexual abuse is an uncomfortable topic for many teachers. Yet every teacher has a moral and legal obligation
to report cases of such abuse. Here are suggestions for
dealing with children who have been abused sexually.

43. Brassard, M.R., Tyler, A.H. and T.J. Kehle. 'Sexually
Abused Children: Identification and Suggestions for
Intervention,' *School Psychology Review*, 12 (Winter
1983) 93-7
Suggests ways to help school psychologists: 1) identify
victims of sexual child abuse; 2) interview a victim
and his/her parents; 3) determine who to notify when
sexual child abuse is suspected; and 4) identify treatment and intervention approaches that are appropriate
in the practice of school psychology. Being able to
identify probable child sexual abuse, reporting it to
the appropriate agency, and subsequently working in
concert with the agency increase the likelihood of
stopping the abuse and helping the child overcome its
detrimental effects.

44. Brassard, M.R., Tyler, A.H. and T.J. Kehle, 'School
Programs to Prevent Intrafamilial Child Sexual Abuse,'
*Child Abuse and Neglect*, 7 (2) 1983, 241-5
Because of the incidence of child sexual abuse the

schools should assume a larger role in the development
of preventive and educational programmes. Topics important for prevention efforts are factual information on
sexual abuse, appropriate and inappropriate touch, the
respective role responsibilities and rights of parents
and children, and a sex education approach that
stresses the values of nonexploitation and discrimina-
tion in the choice of whether to engage in sexual behaviour and the choice of partners.

45. Burgess, A.W. and N. Groth. 'Sexual Victimization of
Children,' in R. Volpe, M. Breton and J. Mitton, eds.
*The Maltreatment of the School Age Child.* Toronto:
Lexington Books, 1980, 79–89
The role of school personnel in dealing with the sexual
victimization is reviewed. The approaches to child
protection are outlined. Suggestions for parents are
also included in this article.

46. Koblinsky, S. and N. Behana. 'Child Sexual Abuse: The
Educator's Role in Prevention, Detection and Intervention,' *Young Children*, 39 (Sept. 1984) 3–15
Educators can play an important role by providing prevention programmes and reporting suspected cases of
sexual abuse. Prevention strategies are discussed, and
a reading and audio-visual resource list is included.

47. Lero, S. 'Needed: Standard Policies on Reporting Suspected Child Abuse in Daycare and Preschool Centers.'
*Journal of Child Care*, 1 (Jan. 1983) 77–86
Lero contends that suspected cases of abuse may go unreported because the professional involved is uncertain
of the legal obligations and procedures. Discussion of
an Ontario study in 1980 which showed half of the head
teachers in daycare programmes suspected abuse. Emphasis on need for standard reporting procedures.

48. Plummer, C.A. *Preventing Sexual Abuse: Activities and
Strategies for Those Working with Children and Adolescents Curriculum Guides for Grades K-6, 7-12, and
Special Populations.* Holmes Beach, Fla.: Learning Publications, 1984
This resource book provides youth workers and educators
with activities which will reduce the chances of young
people becoming sexually victimized. This book is a

valuable resource for educating young people in defin-
itive but tasteful ways.

The recommended approaches were developed, validated,
and refined in social agency and school settings. Where
such techniques have been employed, the success rate
has been high and public response very positive.

49. Riggs, R.S. and R.M. Taylor, 'Incest: The School's
    Role,' *Journal of School Health*, 52 (Nov. 1982) 553-8
    An article for school personnel on incest as part of
    sexual child abuse, including a list of physical and
    behavioural indicators to watch for in children and
    parents. The special role of the school nurse is high-
    lighted.

50. Shore, D.A. 'Sexual Abuse and Sexual Education in
    Child-Caring Institutions,' *Journal of Social Work and
    Human Sexuality*, 1 (Fall-Winter 1982) 171-84
    Over 400,000 children live in residential institutions
    such as treatment centres, temporary and long term
    shelters, detention homes, youth correctional facili-
    ties, centres for the mentally retarded and develop-
    mentally disabled, and group homes; at least an addi-
    tional 400,000 live in foster homes. These children are
    largely voiceless and at the mercy of the adults who
    operate the institutions or agencies, as well as their
    fellow residents.

    If one accepts the basic premise that the institu-
    tionalized are in many respects second class citizens,
    it is not surprising that we are first now turning our
    attention to institutionalized child abuse and neglect.
    Moreover, if a time line of our involvement with the
    problem of child abuse was plotted, it would be pre-
    dictable that the sexual abuse of children in institu-
    tions would be to the far right of the time line.

51. Volpe, R., Breton, M. and J. Mitton. *The Maltreatment
    of the School-Aged Child.* Toronto, Ont.: Lexington
    Books, 1980
    This collection of essays by American and Canadian
    experts on child abuse is a text on the responsibili-
    ties of educators for detection, intervention and pre-
    vention.

52. Williams, B.G. 'Myths and Sexual Abuse: Identification and Elimination,' *The School Counselor*, 29 (Nov. 1981) 103-10 The author discusses the myths related to sexual abuse.

Father-Daughter Incest

53. Alexander, P.C. 'A Systems Theory Conceptualization of Incest,' *Family Process*, 24 (March 1985) 79-88 In this paper, father-daughter incest is examined from the perspective of general systems theory. Three characteristics of an open system - information exchange  with the environment, negentropy, and dynamic homeostasis - are described and examined with respect to the functioning of incestuous families. Two case studies of families with father-daughter incest illustrate the tendency of these families to be more characteristic of the 'closed' end of the continuum. The role of the environment in the origin and maintenance of the incestuous symptom is also examined. Implications for treatement are presented within the context of this theoretical perspective.

54. Boon, C. 'Betrayal of Trust: Father-Daughter Incest,' *Tellus*, 5 (Winter 1984) 17-19 In the spring of 1984 the author prepared a paper on the long-term effects of father-daughter incest, using the results of a survey of past victims she and two other researchers conducted at the Univeristy of Waterloo. Volunteer respondents were recruited through public notices in southern Ontario and may provide a more unbiased representation of incest victims than studies of victims in therapy, hospitals, or correctional institutions.
   The respondents who ranged in age from 18 to 72 years, had stopped having sexual contact with their father or other male caretaker an average of 20 years before completing the questionnaires. On average, sexual abuse had begun at age eight and ended at 13. Over 50 per cent reported that sexual contact had occurred more than once a week; 46 per cent said it had continued for five years or more. Intercourse occurred in less than half the cases. Most victims said the incest had serious long-term effects on their lives.

55. Ford, A.R. 'Breach of Trust: Unmasking the Incest Advocates,' *Healthsharing*, Fall 1982, 10-13 (Women Health Sharing, Box 230, Station M, Toronto, Ont. M6S 4T3)
   In this article the focus is on the phenomenon of father-daughter incest. This kind of incest is by far the most common type. Although the film industry might have us believe otherwise, mother-son incest accounts for only about five per cent of cases of reported incest, according to North American statistics available to date. Sibling incest, where there is not an imbalance of power between those involved, is usually much more benign.

56. Henderson, J. 'Is Incest Harmful?' *Canadian Journal of Psychiatry*, 28 (February 1983) 34-40
   Classically, incest has been considered from both a psychological and sociological point of view to have harmful consequences. Genetic research, though by no means lacking controversy of its own, generally supports the notion that inbreeding has untoward genetic consequences. The psychodynamics of all three parties to father-daughter incest seem to indicate that people who become involved in incestuous behaviour are often psychologically damaged before the act, so that if they show subsequent evidence of psychological impairment the incestuous behaviour can be plausibly viewed as a dysfunctional attempt at solving problems as it can be a cause of subsequent psychopathology.

57. Herman, J.L. *Father-Daughter Incest*. Cambridge, Mass.: Harvard University Press, 1981
   Written from a strongly feminist perspective, this book analyzes incest in terms of definitional issues, prevalence, the victim's trauma and the father's failed responsibility.
   The second part of the book draws on interviews with sixty patients – forty incest victims and twenty women whose fathers had been seductive but not overly incestuous.
   The final section deals with issues of crisis intervention, family treatment, and prosecutions, and includes an appendix reviewing the incest statutes in each of the states in the U.S.

58. Herman, J.L. 'Father-Daughter Incest,' *Professional Psychology*, 12 (Feb. 1981) 76-80
    Examines the issue of incest from the perspective of male dominance. Contends that incest is a tyrannical abuse of power by the father, particularly in families where the mother has been subjugated and the daughter has been socialized into traditionally submissive female roles. Notes that as many as one in ten women report sexual experiences with relatives in childhood and that incest often begins between the ages of six and eleven.

59. Herman, J.L. 'Recognition and Treatment of Incestuous Families,' *Internatinal Journal of Family Therapy*, 5 (Summer 1983) 81-91
    Incest is a major mental health problem, in terms of both prevalence and morbidity. Father-daughter incest constitutes the majority of reported cases. The possibility of incest should be considered in a family which includes a violent father, a disabled mother, a child in an adult maternal role, or an 'acting out' adolescent girl. Intervention requires recognition of the criminal and addictive aspects of the father's behaviour. Active cooperation between mental health professionals and mandated child protective and law enforcement agencies is necessary for effective treatment. Group therapy and affiliated self-help programmes appear to be the treatment modality of choice. Rehabilitation of the family is based upon restoration of the mother-daughter bond as a guarantee of safety for the child.

60. Herman, J.L. and L. Hirschman. 'Families at Risk for Father-Daughter Incest.' *American Journal of Psychiatry* 138 (July 1981) 967-70
    Attempts to identify key characteristics in the family environment which increase the likelihood of incestuous contact between father and daughter.

61. Mey Vander, B.J. and R.L. Neff. 'Adult-Child Incest: A Sample of Substantiated Cases,' *Family Relations*, 33 (Oct. 1984) 549-57
    This paper describes a sample of substantiated cases of adult-child incest. The sample consisted of 15 reports

involving 26 victims. These cases were analyzed and
discussed in relationship to previous studies. The pre-
ponderance of cases were of father-daughter or step/-
foster father-daughter involvement, with biological
father cases the most numerous. The most frequent
source of the initial report was the victim. Emphasis
is placed on replicated and newly identified risk factors including alcohol dependency, spouse abuse, other
(non-sexual) child abuse or neglect, inadequate hous-
ing, social isolation, birth order, and other family
configuration variables.

62. Prince, J. 'Father-Daughter Incest: An Attempt to Maintain the Family and to Meet Human Needs?' *Family and
Community Health*, 4 (Aug. 1981) 35-44
Considers the various psychological and societal factors confronting all members of an incestuous family.
Causes of the overt incestuous activity are identified
and the role of the mother is stressed.

63. Swanson, L. and M.K. Biaggio. 'Therapeutic Perspectives
on Father-Daughter Incest,' *American Journal of
Psychiatry*, 142 (June 1985) 667-74
A literature review related to father-daughter incest
and implications for therapy are presented.

64. Thorman, G. *Incestuous Families*. Springfield, Ill.:
Charles C. Thomas, 1983
The book focuses primarily on father-daughter incest
and only brief mention is made of other forms of incest, although some may be quite common (eg, incestuous
relations among uncles or grandfathers and young children or adolescents, or homosexual incestuous relations). The first three chapters provide an overview of
father-daughter incest both in terms of the scope of
the problem and the internal dynamics of incestuous
families. Additional chapters focus on treatment, prevention and the long-term consequences of incest on
survivors.

Grandparent Incest

65. Goodwin, J., Cormier, L. and J. Owen. 'Grandfather-
granddaughter Incest: A Trigenerational View,' *Child
Abuse & Neglect*, 7 (2) 1983, 163-70

Presents demographic characteristics of grandfather-granddaughter incest perpetrated by 50–65 year old males. All referrals came from mothers of the child victims; six of these mothers had themselves been abused in childhood by the perpetrator. For eight of the 10 perpetrators, multiple child sexual victims were identified in a pattern that suggests facultative pedophilia. Only two of the 18 one-to-18-year-old grandchildren sexually abused by the 10 grandfathers were asymptomatic at the time of the report. Grandchild victims from chaotic families showed educational and behavioral symptoms; those from stable families exhibited fears and phobias. Eight of the 18 grandchildren were victimized by multiple perpetrators. Results cast doubt on the assumption that grandparent incest is a benign form of abuse and indicate that there is some justification for the fears expressed by adult incest victims about visitation between their children and the father-perpetrator.

## Handbooks

66. Canadian Association of Social Work Administrators in Health Facilities. *Domestic Violence Protocol Manual: For Social Workers in Health Facilities*. Ottawa, Ont.: National Clearinghouse on Family Violence, Health and Welfare, Canada, 1985
The phrase domestic violence encompasses all types of abuse that occur in the home: physical and sexual abuse of children and adults, and abuse or neglect of elderly persons. Since victims of these types of abuse often turn to health care facilities for treatment, their contact with the social worker in these settings may be their first genuine opportunity to discuss their experiences. Sensitive interviewing skills are crucial to creating the trust necessary for exploring options.

67. Chisholm, B., ed. *Child Abuse: A Handbook for Social Workers in Ontario*. Toronto, Ont.: Ontario Association of Professional Social Workers, 1983 (185 Bloor St. E., Ste. 701, Toronto, Ont. M4W 3J3)
While the law has meaning for all citizens and residents of Ontario, it has particular implications for members of professional disciplines. It is the intent of this Handbook to assist social workers in settings

other than Children's Aid Socieites in the exercise of
their obligations to the children of this province, not
only as set out in the legislation, and in the manuals
prepared by the Ministry of Community and Social
Services, but in the spirit of the purpose and ethics
of the social work profession.

68. Cooper, S., Lutter, Y. and C. Phelps. *Strategies for
Free Children: A Leader's Guide to Child Assault Prevention.* Columbus, Ohio: Child Assault Prevention Project (CAP), 1983 (P.O. Box 02084, Columbus, Ohio 43202)
This book is a comprehensive step-by-step 'how to'
manual designed for parents, professionals, school
personnel and the general community interested in
setting up a similar programme. It covers everything
from programme philosophy to working out finances, from
dealing with school board and administrative dynamics
to staff 'burnout,' from outlines for adult training
sessions to detailed role-playing situations for children; from how to begin a project to how to achieve
'closure' with a community.

69. Cunningham, M. *Helping the Sexually Abused Child: A
Guide for Foster Parents.* San Rafael, Calif.: Makin
County, Dept of Health and Human Services, 1982
A handbook geared to foster parents who may look after
sexually abused children.

70. Daughherty, L.B. *Why Me? Help for Victims of Child
Sexual Abuse.* Racine, Wis.: Mother Courage Press, 1984
(1533 Illinois St., Racine, WI 53405)
This book was written to be read by victims of child
sexual abuse who are now teenagers or adults. It is
also intended for counsellors or other people who want
to understand and help these victims.

71. Erickson, E.L., McEvoy, A.W., and N.D. Colucci. *Child
Abuse and Neglect: A Guidebook for Educators and
Community Leaders - Second Edition.* Holmes Beach,
Fla.: Learning Publications, 1984
This book is designed to help educators, social service
workers and community leaders develop programmes in
their schools for combatting and preventing child maltreatment. This book deals with programming after educators have become sensitized to the magnitude of child

abuse and neglect. However, becoming aware of maltreatment, wanting to do something about the problem and
having school boards issue school policies are not sufficient to alleviate this undesirable condition.

72. Falconer, N.E. and K. Swift. *Preparing for Practice:
    The Fundamentals of Child Protection*. Toronto, Ont.:
    The Children's Aid Society of Metropolitan Toronto,
    1983
    This manual was prepared for the Metropolitan Toronto
    Children's Aid Society for use by new child welfare
    social workers as an adjunct to their first months of
    job placement. The material is presented in what the
    authors call a 'user friendly' style. The result is a
    handy, concise and easily-read handbook on child wel-
    fare practice, with a 'how to' tone in lecture note
    format. A section on sexual abuse is included.

73. Faller, K.C., ed. *Social Work with Abused and Neglected
    Children: A Manual of Interdisciplinary Practice*. New
    York, N.Y.: Free Press, 1981
    Incidents of child abuse and neglect are being reported
    in increasing numbers. More than ever before, social
    workers need to know how, when, and with which other
    professionals to intervene in these cases.
      *Social Work with Abused and Neglected Children* is a
    joint work of IPCAN (the University of Michigan Inter-
    disciplinary Project on Child Abuse and Neglect), de-
    signed to train professionals to work collaboratively
    in diagnosing and managing cases of abuse and neglect.
      Nineteen chapters by social workers, lawyers, physi-
    cians, psychologists, and psychiatrists who work with
    maltreated children cover the wide range of approaches
    professionals may take to work effectively, and in co-
    operation with others, in the best interest of the child.

74. Marois, M.R., Messier, C. and L.A. Perreault. *Incest:
    Three or More's A Crowd 'Learning to Help them'*.
    Québec, Qué.: Ministry of Justice, Committee on the
    Protection of Youth, 1984
    A guide to dealing with the problems of sexual abuse of
    children.

75. Mills, D.J. *Child Sexual Assault: A Guide for Parents*.
    Saskatoon, Sask.: Sexual Assault and Information

Centre, 1984 (302–115 2nd Ave. N., Saskatoon, Sask.
S7K 2B1)
This booklet gives information about sexual abuse to
parents.

76. Moore, J.G. *The ABC of Child Abuse Work.* Brookfield,
    Vt.: Gower, 1985 (Old Post Rd., Brookfield, Vt. 05036)
    This book is a basic primer for new workers about the
    causes of physical injury and sexual and emotional
    abuse of children. It offers step–by–step guidance on
    how to offer real help. Numerous case studies from day
    to day practice are used to enable the reader to un-
    derstand why children are physically or sexually abused
    or become emotionally damaged by marital violence. The
    author offers many positive, basic and detailed sugges-
    tions about what can actually be done in situations
    which are often fraught with anxiety. The feeling
    stirred up by family violence which can often render
    social workers professionaly impotent are addressed
    directly, in the context of methods aimed at giving
    children and parents involved a skilled and sensitive
    service. A full description of face–to–face work with
    abused children is also presented.

77. Nova Scotia Dept of Education. *What Every Teacher
    Should Know About Child Abuse and Neglect.* Halifax,
    N.S., 1985 (P.O. Box 578, Halifax, N.S. B3J 2S9)
    This booklet gives the teacher some information about
    child abuse, including sexual abuse.

78. Sgroi, S.M. *Handbook of Clinical Intervention in Child
    Sexual Abuse.* Lexington, Mass.: Lexington Books, 1982
    This book attempts to convey a coherent and cohesive
    perspective on the state of the art in child–sexual–
    abuse intervention in 1981. The observations, opinions,
    and recommendations expressed are based on clinical ex-
    perience and the considerable experience of colleagues,
    the contributing authors. Most of the chapters examine
    the various aspects of intervention and present infor-
    mation in a 'here–is–how–we–do–it' format.
       The aim in all of the chapters is to emphasize the
    practical rather than the theoretical aspects of inter-
    vention. Whenever possible, case examples are used to
    illustrate the points made and the approach recommended.

79. Stevenson, J. *A Childhood for Every Child: A Handbook on Child Abuse for Ontario Teachers*. Toronto, Ont.: Ontario Teachers' Federation, 1984 (1260 Bay St., Toronto, Ont. M5R 2B5)
    This book is about action. It is a 'How To' book on:
    - how to *recognize* possible instances of child abuse;
    - how to *investigate* them;
    - how to handle some of the *distress* such cases will; inevitably bring up for you;
    - how to *speak* to the child, the parent(s), the authorities;
    - how to *report* a case;
    - how to *support* the child and his/her siblings in your school as a case unfolds.

80. Thomas, H. *Child Abuse: Neglect and Deprivation: A Handbook for Ontario Nurses*. Toronto, Ont.: Registered Nurses Association of Ontario, 1983
    It is hoped that those who read this handbook will find:
    - increased knowledge, useful in the treatment of abused, neglected and deprived children and their families;
    - satisfaction in recognizing their abilities to deal with abusing, neglecting and depriving families;
    - strength to recognize their limitations in practice and to make realistic plans to resolve them;
    - energy to continue treating these families;
    - compassion and sensitivity to provide these families with a sense of hope for the future;
    - enthusiasm to function as an effective advocate for these families;
    - perseverance to inspire themselves and others to continue to ask questions in the area of child abuse, neglect and deprivation and to seek answers - scientifically.

Historical Background of Sexual Abuse

81. Foucalt, M. *The History of Sexuality - Volume I: An Introduction*. New York, N.Y.: Vintage Books, 1980
    In his historical overview, the author discusses incest and psychoanalysis (pp. 129-30).

82. Fox, R. *The Red Lamp of Incest*. New York, N.Y.:
    Dutton, 1980
    This book is a summation of Fox's major contributions
    to the anthropological literature on incest, set in the
    context of his growing interest in viewing human social
    behaviour from the perspective of evolutionary biology.
    He disposes early on the idea that incest avoidance is
    something that sets man apart from the rest of the
    animal kingdom, citing data from field studies and also
    making the general point that close inbreeding would
    tend to nullify the advantage that a sexually reproduc-
    ing species has over those that follow the more direct
    route of asexual reproduction. Humans may be unique in
    having rules about incest – as they are in having rules
    generally – but they are not unique in exhibiting in-
    cest avoidance.
       Among the other preconceived notions Fox seeks to
    dispel is that of a universal horror of incest among
    human societies, or even a universal taboo. Noting
    societies in which unions between close relatives are
    permitted or enjoined, he documents varying cultural
    attitudes towards incest, which range from horror to
    ridicule to incomprehension.

83. Gordon, L. and P. O'Keefe, 'Incest as a form of family
    violence: evidence from historical case records, *Journal of
    Marriage and the Family*, 46 (Feb. 1984) 27-34
    In the course of a study of family violence and its
    social control, drawing on case records from Boston-
    area social service agencies during the period 1880-
    1960, the authors found a random sample of 502 that had
    been created included 50 cases of incest. The authors
    have examined these incest cases individually in the
    light of recent incest scholarship; findings presented
    are seen to corroborate certain findings of recent
    clinical studies on incest, notably concerning its
    frequency and the predominance of father-daughter in-
    cest as a social problem. The historical cases also
    suggest that such incest usually is coercive, and is
    thus accurately considered a form of family violence.
    Comparison of incestuous families with those experi-
    encing other forms of family violence shows that the
    former are by no means more stressed, nor the indiv-
    iduals in them more pathological. Also, incest victims
    are no more willing participants than are child vic-
    tims of nonsexual abuse.

84. McCarthy, B. 'Incest and Psychotherapy,' *Irish Journal
    of Psychotherapy*, 1 (Sept. 1982) 11–16
    Contends that Freud found the idea of incest personally
    disturbing, reflecting possibilities of repressed actual
    incest experiences in his own childhood, and incestuous
    dangers in his relationship with his own children. His
    later abandonment of the idea of widespread seduction
    of children, and its replacement by the theory of wish
    fulfilment rather than real experience, resulted in
    his theory of infantile sexuality, incestuous wishes,
    the Oedipus complex, and the formation of the superego.
    Henceforth, psychoanalysis virtually ignored incest as
    a reality. Interest shifted to the defenses against
    acting out incestuous wishes, both in individual patho-
    logy and social anthropology. It is argued that locat-
    ing the theme of incest in the world of unconscoius
    fantasy deflected attention away from the reality of
    incest and delayed the discovery of sexual abuse with-
    in the family. Three case examples of adults who were
    child incest victims are presented, and the management
    of cases of sexual abuse is discussed.

85. Schultz, L.G. 'Child Sexual Abuse in Historical
    Perspective,' *Journal of Social Work and Human
    Sexuality*, 1 (Fall–Winter 1982) 21–36
    The history of childhood in Western societies makes for
    disheartening reading, but when combined with childhood
    sexual development over time, it becomes one of unadul-
    tered ugliness. The historical evolution of childhood
    and sexuality is characterized by superstition, unreason-
    able fears, folklore, fanacticism and medical sadism. The
    discovery of 'childhood' and 'adolescence' as distinct
    from adulthood were a late invention. The protection of
    childrens' and adolescents' sexual integrity emerged
    slowly and incrementally over several hundred years in
    both criminal law and in protective social services. This
    short history attempts to pull together significant bits
    of historical evidence from the past and weaves them into
    a coarse framework. The reader is cautioned as to histor-
    ical accuracy, due to the sparcity of evidence, unfilled
    time gaps and the need for synthesis stretching.

86. Scott, D. 'Incest – a matter of models,' *Australian
    Social Work*, 36 (4), 1983, 23–30
    The purpose of this discussion is to stimulate debate
    within the social work profession about incest. The

literature on the origins and functions of the incest taboo is reviewed, and the historical process by which incest came to be the subject of legislation is described. The psychoanalytic and family systems models of incest are supported, and preliminary guidelines for the psychosocial assessment of families in which incest occurs are offered.

87. Serrano, A.C. and D.W. Gunzburger, 'An Historical Perspective on Incest,' *International Journal of Family Therapy*, 5 (Summer 1983) 70–80
Incest has been documented in most civilizations and for as long as can be remembered. This article begins with a brief historical overview of incest across cultures and times. The second part includes a review of several theories that place the significance of the incest taboo in an historical continuum.

88. Shepher, J. *Incest: A Biosocial View*. New York, N.Y.: Academic Press, 1983
This book illuminates the question of the origin of the universal human taboo against incest. Shepher presents the sociobiological theory of incest regulations in the only book in the last 100 years to survey the entire literature and to synthesize previous approaches in light of one theory.
   After introducing the sociobiological theory and the complicated methodological questions inherent in investigating the concept of incest, the author examines the development of biosocial thinking on the subject from Westermarck to Robin Fox. His own evidence – together with Wolf's research in Taiwan – leads to the central chapter which presents a genetic and mathematical model of the sociobiological theory of incest. In the remaining chapters, Shepher discusses the conflict between his sociobiological theory of incest and the classical theories of Freud, Parsons, Murdock, Tylor, Lévi-Strauss, and White.

Homosexual Incest

89. Kaslow, F., Haupt, D., Arce, A.A. and J. Werblowsky, 'Homosexual Incest,' *Psychiatric Quarterly*, 53 (Fall 1981) 184–93

Observes that there is a dearth of cases reported on
homosexual incest in the literature. Provides two case
studies of sibling homosexual incest and analyzes the
psychodynamics of the patients. Notes that these incest
victims may exhibit severe psychopathology including
suicidal behaviour. Recommends a treatment which includes sessions with members of the family of origin as
well as several sessions with the family of procreation.

90. Myers, M.F. 'Homosexuality, Sexual Dysfunction, and
Incest in Male Identical Twins,' *Canadian Journal of
Psychiatry*, 27 (1982) 144-7
Reports a unique case of incestuous activity between
two male identical twins. Both suffered from a variety
of sexual dysfunctions and found it difficult to live
apart. Individual and conjoint therapy was used to
treat both twins. Results of tests to determine
physical and psychological similarities are presented.

Incest and Alcoholism

91. Barnard, C.P. 'Alcoholism and Incest: Improving Diagnostic Comprehensiveness,' *International Journal of
Family Therapy*, 5 (Summer 1983), 136-44
This article is designed to underscore the similarities
in characteristics between alcoholic and incestuous
family operations. Hopefully, readers will develop a
more acute appreciation and understanding of the frequency of occurrence of both of these behaviours in the
same family. The author contends that too often alcoholism will be diagnosed, while the incest is diagnos-
tically missed or vice versa. To best insure that recidivism of either the alcohol or incest can be avoided,
the author believes it is important to comprehensively
diagnose and then treat appropriately.

Incest: Feminist Views

92. Armstrong, L. 'The Cradle of Sexual Politics: Incest'
in M. Kirkpatrick, ed. *Women's Sexual Experience: Ex-
plorations of the Dark Continent*. New York, N.Y.:
Plenum Press, 1982, 109-25
More research is certainly needed, but not on why
individual fathers do this, nor on the profile of the

incestuous father, nor on the profile of the incestuous
family – not on whether *we* all become prostitutes or
drug addicts, but on the core, dramatic issue: What is
the nature of the powerful need on the part of so many
men to preserve the permission to exploit their children sexually?

93. McNaron, T.A. and Y. Morgan. *Voices in the Night: Women
Speaking About Incest.* Minneapolis, Minn.: Cleis Press,
1982
A collection of feminist prose and poetry concerning
incest is presented. Though incest may occur in the
life of one out of three women, there is a silence
about incest and its effects. The silence of women who
have been incest victims is self-imposed. These victims
feel shame at having been abused by those who were supposed to love them. The horror of that abuse and shame
turns inward as the victim tries to learn what she has
done wrong and why this is happening to her.

Incest: The Media

94. DeMott, B. 'The Pro-Incest Lobby,' *Psychology Today*, 13
(March 1980) 11–16
A critical article which deals with the recent interest
related to incest in the popular media. The author
feels that incest is being given a positive view by the
media.

Incest: Mothers of Victims

95. Dietz, C. and J. Craft, 'Family Dynamics of Incest: A
New Perspective,' *Social Casework*, 61 (Dec. 1980) 602–9
This paper explores the role of the mother in incestuous families, as perceived by 200 child protection service workers in Iowa, and examines the attitudes of
these workers toward the mother. An additional goal is
to determine whether parallels and possible connections
exist between incest and wife abuse.
   The authors review literature which argues that the
real abuser in an incestuous family is the mother. By
frustrating her husband sexually, failing to support
her daughter emotionally, or foisting her maternal
duties and responsibilities onto her daughter, she
engineers the incestuous relationship.

96. McIntyre, K. 'Role of mothers in father-daughter
    incest: a feminist analysis,' *Social Work*, 26 (Nov.
    1981) 462-6
    Much of the current theory of incest and approaches to
    treatment ignore the impact of a patriarchal society
    and culture in promoting and encouraging incestuous as-
    sault. The author examines sexist assumptions about the
    roles of family members, on which basis the mother –
    instead of the actual offender – is usually blamed for
    the assault. He presents an analysis of incest that
    seeks to help professionals empower the victims of male
    violence.

97. Myer, M.H. 'A New Look at Mothers of Incest Victims,'
    *Journal of Social Work and Human Sexuality*, 3 (Winter
    1984-Spring 1985) 47-58
    Mothers of incest victims are labeled passive, depen-
    dent, masochistic, as unable to deal with their own
    history of victimization, and as abdicating their role
    of wife and mother to the victimized daughter. A study
    of 43 women suggests that few mothers of incest victims
    fits this description. The findings have important im-
    plications for intervention and treatment.

98. Zuelzer, M.B. and R.E. Reposa. 'Mothers in Incestuous
    Families,' *International Journal of Family Therapy*, 5
    (Summer 1983) 98-110
    Based on the premise that mothers in father-daughter
    incest families are pivotal in the incestuous bond,
    this article considers the incestuous mother's per-
    sonality dynamics and role within the context of
    parent-child nuclear and extended family interaction.
    Such fundamental issues as separation-individuation,
    identification, and fear of intimacy are addressed from
    a developmental perspective. Patterns of functioning of
    mothers who are both victims and colluders are high-
    lighted, followed by treatment implications.

Incest: Overview

99. Cormier, B.M. and I.K. Cooper. 'Incest in Contemporary
    Society: Legal and Clinical Management' in D.A.
    Galbraith, ed. *The Family*. London, Ont.: Children's
    Psychiatric Research Institute, 1980 (20th Annual
    Symposium) 168-202

A comprehensive paper dealing with the legal and clinical aspects of incest in Canada.

100. Gelinas, D.J. 'The Persisting Negative: Effects of Incest,' *Psychiatry*, 46 (Nov. 1983) 312-32
This paper identifies and explains the underlying, persisting negative effects of incest and then reviews the characteristic 'disguised presentation' to assist the clinician in recognizing when a patient might be an undisclosed incest victim.

101. Lieske, A.M. 'Incest: An Overview,' *Perspectives in Psychiatric Care*, 19 (March-April 1981) 59-63
Professional attitudes, common misconceptions, the cyclic nature, and causative factors in relation to incest are discussed. Incest reflects pathology in the family unit and psychologically involves most if not all of the family. The father-daughter relationship is most common and usually is nonviolent. The female incest victim usually appears more mature than she actually is, and is often responsible for child care and housekeeping. Self-destructive tendencies of incest victims include suicide attempts, truancy, runaway behaviour, chemical abuse, and promiscuity.

102. Renvoize, J. *Incest: A Family Pattern*. London: Routledge & Kegan Paul, 1982
The author bases this book both on her British experience of the treatment of victims of incest, and interviews with key figures in treatment programmes in the United States. In her introduction Renvoize notes, with disapproval that, 'The father or stepfather or whoever the perpetrator may be very often claims that 'no harm has been done.' And underneath the public desire not to discuss incest there occasionally lies the same feeling, that when it comes down to it, what are we actually making a fuss about? Is it so awful, after all, as long as there was no violence, no pain?'
    The author's case histories make it clear that harm is very frequently done by child sexual abuse, and that the deep psychological scars which result do not heal quickly or easily. She concludes in quoting with approval Henry Kempe, one of the pioneers in identifying sexual abuse of children as a major social problem.

103. Ruch, L.O. and S.M. Chandler. 'The Crisis Impact of
     Sexual Assault on Three Victim Groups: Adult Rape
     Victims, Child Rape Victims, and Incest Victims,'
     *Journal of Social Service Research*, 5 (1/2) 1982,
     83–100
     The traumatizing effect of rape and other forms of
     sexual assault on the victim has been documented in a
     variety of recent studies. The diversity of these
     studies with respect to their samples, data collection
     methods, and measurement procedures makes if difficult
     to specify with precision (1) the effect of rape on
     adult vs child victims, and (2) the effect of rape vs
     incestuous assault on child victims. The purpose of
     this research was to develop and apply a standardized
     assault impact assessment to a sample of victims ad-
     mitted to a rape crisis treatment centre. Three compar-
     ison groups compose the focus of this study: adult rape
     victims, child rape victims, and child incest victims.
     This article deals with the levels of trauma stemming
     from sexual assault in these groups and the implica-
     tions of these findings for sexual assault treatment
     centres.

104. Silver, R.L., Boon, C., and M.H. Stones. 'Searching for
     meaning in misfortune: making sense of incest,' *Journal
     of Social Issues*, 39 (2) 1983, 81–101
     A major component of many disturbing life events is
     that they frequently destroy the victim's perception of
     living in a world that is well-ordered and meaningful.
     Much research has suggested that in the wake of such
     outcomes, the search for meaning is a common and adap-
     tive process. The authors investigate the validity of
     that claim by examining data from a recent study of 77
     adult women who as children were all victims of father-
     daughter incest. There seems to be no clearcut answer
     as to whether the women in this sample were able to
     find meaning in their victimization; more than half of
     the subjects who were actively searching for meaning an
     average of twenty years after the incest had ended re-
     ported that they could make no sense of it whatsoever.
     The authors contend that the ruminations and remembran-
     ces that are part of the search for meaning serve an
     adaptive function in that they are likely to be the
     means by which individuals begin to gain control over

and make sense of their experience – but even finding meaning does not seem to end the search or the ruminations.

105. Taubman, S. 'Incest in Context,' *Social Work*, 29 (Jan.-Feb. 1984) 35–40
The prevailing constricted concept of incest has been shaped by avoidance, denial, compartmentalization, and blaming. This article presents a more comprehensive view of the societal, cultural, familial, and personality factors that form the context of people at risk for incest and associated problems. The consequences of incest and the causal context of incest are summarized. An ecosystems approach to interventions is described.

106. Williams, G.J. and J. Money, eds. *Traumatic Abuse and Neglect of Children at Home*. Baltimore, Md.: Johns Hopkins University Press, 1980
Part seven of this book of edited papers contains five papers dealing with various aspects of incest.

Incest and Remarriage

107. Perlmutter, L., Engel, T. and C.J. Sager.'The Incest Taboo: Loosened Sexual Boundaries in Remarried Families,' *Journal of Sex and Marital Therapy*, 8 (2) 1982, 83–96
Household sexual abuse is reported here as a dysfunction in some remarried families with a child who presents problems of depression, suicidal gestures, adolescent rebelliousness, or poor school achievement. Common dynamics of the family and each family member are explored and treatment issues are discussed. A child's ability to admit abuse is a function of the therapist's comfort in hearing it, ability to deal with anger, and need to exercise control. Various forms of sexual abuses and their treatment are illustrated with case histories.

108. Russell, D.E.H. 'The Prevalence and Seriousness of Incestuous Abuse: Stepfathers vs Biological Fathers,' *Child Abuse and Neglect*, 8 (1) 1984, 15–22
Analysis of interviews obtained from a random sample of 930 adult women in San Francisco revealed that 17 per cent or one out of approximately every six women who

had a stepfather as a principal figure in her childhood
years, was sexually abused by him. The comparable
figures for biological fathers were two per cent or one
out of approximately 40 women. In addition, when a distinction was made between *Very Serious Sexual Abuse*
(including experiences ranging from forced penile-
vaginal penetration to non-forceful attempted fellatio,
cunnilingus, and anal intercourse) and other less serious forms, 47 per cent of the cases of sexual abuse by
stepfathers were at the *Very Serious* level of violation
compared with 26 per cent by biological fathers. Possible explanations for these startling discrepancies
are discussed, and some of the implications for remarriage are considered.

## Incidence of Sexual Abuse

109. Lobb, M.L. and G.M. Strain. 'Temporal Patterns of Child
     Abuse and Neglect Reporting: Implications for Personnel
     Scheduling,' *Child Welfare*, 63 (Sept.-Oct. 1984) 453-466
     A year of child abuse and neglect data from the Texas
     Department of Human Resources in Dallas, Texas, were
     investigated to determine if periodic effects exist in
     the patterns of child abuse and neglect reporting. Re-
     sults are discussed in terms of efficient scheduling of
     personnel and anticipated workloads.

110. McIvor, D.L. and D. Evans. 'Incest Victims: The
     Adults,' *Canadian Journal of Psychiatric Nursing*, 24
     (Jan.-Feb. 1983) 11-12
     The long-lasting consequences of incest in the lives of
     adults who were childhood victims of incest are de-
     scribed, and treatment strategies for such adult incest
     victims are reviewed. It is estimated that only 20 per
     cent of incest occurrences are ever reported. The most
     common dynamic involved in not reporting the experience
     is: 1) the experience has been mentally blocked from
     memory; 2) the adult assumes guilt for the experience
     and is too ashamed to talk about it; and 3) the adult
     continues to fear the impact upon family harmony by re-
     porting the experience at a later date.

111. Mrazek, P.J., Lynch, M.A. and A. Bentovim. 'Sexual
     Abuse of Children in the United Kingdom,' *Child Abuse &
     Neglect*, 7 (2) 1983, 147-53

Circulated questionnaires to 622 family doctors, police
surgeons, pediatricians, and child psychiatrists to determine the frequency and nature of child sexual abuse
in the U.K. At least three out of 1,000 children (defined as under 15 years of age) are currently being
recognized as sexually abused sometime during their
childhood. The majority of cases reported involved actual or attempted intercourse, and 74 per cent of the
perpetrators were known to the child. Family disturb-
ance was noted in 56 per cent of the cases. The most
common outcome (43%) was criminal prosecution of the
perpetrator. Area review committees had no clear policy
for the management of sexual abuse. It is concluded
that before it is possible to protect children and to
develop therapeutic services for the family, it will be
necessary to acknowledge that sexual abuse is part of
the child abuse spectrum.

112. Russell, D.E.H. 'The Incidence and Prevalence of Intrafamilial and Extrafamilial Sexual Abuse of Female
Children,' *Child Abuse & Neglect*, 7 (2) 1983, 133–46
Attempted to estimate the prevalence of intrafamilial
and extrafamilial sexual abuse of female children based
on interview data on at least one experience as reported by 930 urban women. Findings indicate the following:
1) intrafamilial sexual abuse was experienced by 16 per
cent of the SS before the age of 18 years and by 12 per
cent of the SS before 14 years of age; 2) extrafamilial
sexual abuse was experienced by 31 per cent of the SS
before the age of 18 years and by 20 per cent before 14
years of age; and 3) when both categories of sexual
abuse were combined, sexual abuse occurred among 38 per
cent of the SS before 18 years of age and among 28 per
cent before 14 years of age. Only two per cent of the
cases of intrafamilial and 6 per cent of the cases of
extrafamilial child sexual abuse were ever reported to
the police. Findings underscore the need to recognize
the magnitude of the problem of child sexual abuse and
to prevent it.

113. Wilson, J., Thomas, D. and L. Schlette. 'The Silent
Screams: Recognizing Abused Children,' *Education*, 104
(Fall 1983) 100–3
Presents information about types of child abuse and
symptoms by which helping professionals may identify

abused children. As many as 100,000 children per year
in the U.S. are victims of child, physical or sexual
abuse or neglect. One means of intervening with this
problem is early identification of symptoms of abuse or
neglect. It is suggested that educators, who work with
children on a day-to-day basis, are in a good position
to observe physical manifestations of abuse such as
bruises in various stages of healing or to note behavioral indicators such as withdrawal or fear of
adults. Guidelines on how to report abuse are presented.

Legal Aspects of Sexual Abuse

114. Besherov, D., ed. *Child Abuse and Neglect: Interpreting the Law in Canada*. New York, N.Y.: Child Welfare
League of America, 1985
This is the single most comprehensive description of
how the courts and the Children's Aid Societies interpret and apply Ontario's *Child Welfare Act* and related
statutes. A product of a 1982 seminar on Child Protection and Canadian Law held at the Osgoode Hall Law
School, this volume offers a unique analysis and exploration of all the major forms of child abuse and
neglect, from physical abuse to abandonment; criminal
prosecutions of parents; Society and Crown wardship
decisions; civil and criminal liability for failing to
report and in child protection generally. On each
specific topic there is background information, relevant statutes and court decisions, analyses of the
factors that seem to guide agency and judicial decision
making, and special evidentiary consideration.

115. Boyle, C. *Sexual Assault*. Toronto: Carswell, 1984
This monograph deals with the Canadian legal aspects
related to sexual assault.

116. Bulkley, J., ed. *Child Sexual Abuse and the Law*.
Washington, D.C.: American Bar Association, National
Legal Resource Center for Child Advocay and Protection,
second ed., 1982
A collection of articles designed to be practical
rather than philosophical in nature, and geared toward
an audience of attorneys, legislators, prosecutors,
clinicians and programme planners. The focus is on

intrafamily child sexual abuse. The first half of the
book is given over to comparative (state by state)
analysis of laws which relate to child sexual abuse.
Of greater interest outside these jurisdictions are the
remaining articles, which deal with key issues of corroboration of sexual victimization, expert testimony,
competency of children as witnesses, and attempts to
prepare and protect child victim/witnesses.

117. Conte, J.R. 'The Justice System and Sexual Abuse of
Children,' *Social Service Review*, 58 (Dec. 1984) 556-68
One of the most controversial issues dividing professionals working with sexually abused children is the
role of the justice system in responding to these
cases. From a social work perspective, this controversy
is fueled in part by misconceptions about the problem
of sexual abuse of children. This article takes a critical look at common beliefs about sexual abuse of children, and discusses the initial treatment needs of
these cases and how the justice system can be helpful
in meeting these needs.

118. Eaurer, H. 'Preparation of the Sexually Abused Child
for Court Testimony,' *Bulletin of the American Academy
of Psychiatry and the Law*, 11 (3) 1983, 287-9
Argues that in the case of a sexually abused child, the
main purpose of court intervention is not protection of
the child but conviction and punishment of the offender. In such trials, children play an important role as
witnesses that decide the guilt or innocence of a person who is usually well known to the child and frequently a close relative.

119. Horowitz, A.N. 'When to Intervene in Cases of Suspected
Incest,' *Social Casework*, 63 (June 1982) 374-5
This brief article questions a position taken by Joseph
Goldstein, Anna Freud, and Albert J. Solnit in their
recent book *Before the Best Interests of the Child*.
Their thesis is that a criminal conviction or an ac-
quittal on the basis of insanity should constitute the
only grounds for state intervention in cases of suspected sexual involvement between a parent and child.
Although the authors acknowledge the harm done to a
child's development by sexual involvement with a parent, they believe that this damage is exacerbated by

subjecting the family to an investigation and the possibility of a placement process. They argue that the
harm caused by intervention can be greater than that
caused in the absence of intervention.

120. Hoskins, J.G. 'The Rise and Fall of the Corroboration
Rule in Sexual Offence Cases,' *Canadian Journal of
Family Law*, 4 (Oct. 1983) 173-214
The author sets out the three rules of evidence which
set the trials of sexual offences apart from other
criminal proceedings. Bill C-127, which amended the
Criminal Code with respect to sexual offences in Jan.
1983, either abrogates the rules or severely restricts
their effect. This paper examines the implications of
one of these rules, the corroboration rule.

121. Krieger, M.J. and J. Robbins. 'The Adolescent Incest
Victim and the Judicial System,' *American Journal of
Orthopsychiatry*, 55 (July 1985) 419-25
The effect on the adolescent incest victim of contact
with the judicial system is reviewed, and the victim's
sense of insignificance, hopelessness, and guilt is
noted. A conceptual framework is offered to aid clinicians in their work with incest victims, and suggestions are made for case management.

122. McCarthy, L.M. 'Investigation of Incest: Opportunity to
Motivate Families to Seek Help,' *Child Welfare*, 60
(Dec. 1981) 679-87
Incest, like other forms of sexual abuse, is a criminal
act that society treats ambiguously. Victims are doubly
victimized by being subjected to disbelief on the part
of those who should protect them. Presented here is a
model for investigation that not only leads to protection for the victim and prosecution for the perpetrat-
or, but guides the family to take steps toward resolving their problem.

123. Ordway, D.P. 'Reforming Judicial Procedures for
Handling Parent-Child Incest,' *Child Welfare*, 62 (Jan.-
Feb. 1983) 68-75
Three major shortcomings of current procedures in
handling cases of parent-child incest are outlined.
Ordway proposes alterntives to the trauma now forced
upon children at the pre-trial and trial stages. He

also recognizes the legal argumens that would be
mounted against his suggested reform.

124. Peterson, S.K. 'Sexual Abuse of Children - Washington's
New Hearsay Exception,' *Washington Law Review*, 58
(Nov. 1983), 813-29
In 1982, the Washington state legislature adopted a new
exception to the hearsay rule for criminal prosecutions
involving the sexual abuse of children. This new exception is Washington's first hearsay exception that gives
the trial court discretion to determine whether an out-
of-court statement is trustworthy. Under the exception,
a statement made by a child under 10 years describing
an act of sexual contact performed with or on the child
by another is admissible if several conditions are
met.

125. Pirro, J.F. 'The Prosecution and Defence of Child
Sexual Assault,' in *The Prosecution and Defence of Sex
Crimes*, New York, N.Y.: Matthew Bender & Company, Inc.,
1984, chap. 9 (235 E. 4th St., New York, N.Y. 10017)
An Assistant District Attorney discusses some of the
problems that might be encountered in the prosecution
and defense of the crime of child sexual assault.

126. Rogers, C.M. 'Child Sexual Abuse and the Courts:  Preliminary Findings,' *Journal of Social Work and Human
Sexuality*, 1 (Fall-Winter 1982) 145-54
Sexual victimization of children, including incest,
rape, and other forms of sexual molestation, constitutes a social problem of major proportions in the
United States. Estimates regarding the incidence of
such sexual victimization vary greatly depending upon
the study setting, the definitional criteria, and the
methodology used for collecting such information. Most
studies however would suggest that perhaps 200,000 to
400,000 children are sexually victimized every year in
the United States. Some retrospective studies would
suggest that the incidence is higher still with one of
every five girls and one of every ten boys or one of
every three children being sexually victimized at least
once during their childhood.
   Sexual victimization of children constitutes a major
social problem not only due to its high frequency of
occurrence but also due to its overall impact on the

child victim and her or his family. Studies suggest
that sexual victimization as a child may be related to
later difficulties in psychosocial adjustment including
drug abuse, juvenile delinquency, juvenile prostitution, adult clinical depression and similar difficulties. In addition, numerous reports attest to the immediate deleterious psychosocial effects of such victimization on children.

127. Savage, C.J. 'Linkages between Child Sexual Abuse and
Later Delinquent or Criminal Behaviour: What is Known?
Victoria, B.C.: Ministry of Attorney General, Jan. 1984
This paper starts with a statement of current belief:
'It has become a truism that a strong linkage exists
between sexual abuse in childhood and later delinquent
or criminal behaviour,' and sets out to examine the extent to which that linkage is documented in the literature. Savage finds that the evidence is very limited.
However, she does not fall into the trap of arguing
that, because no strong linkage can be proved on available evidence, we should downplay the argument. Rather,
she suggests further research to disentangle various
factors that may be at issue.

128. Serrano, A.C. and D.W. Gunzburger. 'Incest and Professional Boundaries: Confidentiality Versus Mandatory
Reporting,' *International Journal of Family Therapy*, 5
(Summer 1983) 145-9
The mandatory reporting of an incest case by a mental
health professional, sets in motion a chain of events
which raise conflict for all involved. Typically, attorneys, the courts, health service providers, as well
as primary treatment teams become involved. This article discusses some of the relevant dilemmas that are
raised by the personal and professional mandatory report of incest.

129. Stone, L.E., Tyler, R.P.T. and J.J. Mead. 'Law Enforcement Officers as Investigators and Therapists in Child
Sexual Abuse: A Training Model,' *Child Abuse and
Neglect*, 8 (1) 1984, 75-82
Law enforcement officers, often the first professionals
to come in contact with a victim of child sexual abuse,
can either increase or decrease the traumatic impact on
the child and the family at the time of disclosure. The

model for a training programme for police officers in
handling cases of child sexual abuse outlined in this
paper is divided into three sections. The first part is
directed towards theoretical issues involved in this
problem, including an explanation of the history and
background of sexual abuse of children by adults and of
the difference in the dynamics of extra- and intrafamilial sexual abuse. The second part consists of a
detailed explanation of different types of sex offenses
and of standard physical examinations of sexual abuse
victims. Graded slides of physical trauma geared towards wound identification are paired with relaxation
exercises. The third section focuses on special consid-
erations when interviewing sexually abused children.
The difference between interviewing and interrogation,
specific questioning techniques, and the use of video-
tape is explained. Each part of this training procedure
is followed by a question and answer period and small
group discussions for the purpose of encouraging disclosure and better understanding of the officers' personal reactions to cases of child sexual abuse.

130. Weiss, E.H. and R.F. Berg. 'Child Psychiatry and Law –
Child Victims of Sexual Assault: Impact of Court
Procedures,' *Journal of the American Academy of Child
Psychiatry*, 21 (5) 1982, 513–18
Discusses the role of mental health professionals in
helping victims of sexual abuse cope with the legal
system at a time when they are most psychologically
vulnerable. Several methods are suggested to assist the
clinician to help both the victim and the victim's
family.

131. Zefran, J., Riley, H.F., Andersen, W.O., Curtis, J.H.,
Jackson, L.M., Kelly, P.H., McGury, E.T. and M.K.
Suriano. 'Management and Treatment of Child Sexual Abuse
Cases in a Juvenile Court Setting,' *Journal of Social
Work and Human Sexuality*, 1 (Fall–Winter 1982) 155–70
The number of child sexual abuse treatment programmes
has been increasing in the past few years. The Juvenile
Court of Cook County, the oldest Juvenile Court in the
country (established in 1899), became a part of this
trend with the establishment of its programme, the
Special Services Unit for the Treatment of Child Sexual
Abuse. This article provides a discussion of the case

management, legal, and therapeutic issues involved in
the handling of child sexual abuse cases at a juvenile
court. The article is based, in part, on data describing the experiences gained in providing service to a
sample (N = 55 families) of sexually abusing families
referred to the Court's Special Services Unit during
the first nine months of 1980.

## Medical Aspects Related to Sexual Abuse

132. Connell, H.M. 'The Paediatrician and the Sexually
     Abused Child,' *Australian Paediatric Journal*, 16 (March
     1980) 49-52
     Sexual abuse is an aspect of cruelty to children that
     merits greater scientific attention. It has potential
     for damaging the mental health of the victim and may
     result in intergenerational repetiton of abusive phe-
     nomena. The pediatrician is in a position to detect
     children at risk and may be able to intervene. The three
     most common types of sexual abuse are: 1) single sexual
     attacks, which may be accompanied by physical violence;
     2) sexual exploitation of children for financial gain;
     and 3) longstanding sexual relationships, which
     generally involve a female child and a father figure.

133. Ellerstein, N. ed. *Child Abuse and Neglect: A Medical
     Reference*. Toronto, Ont.: John Wiley and Sons, 1981
     The chapters are sensibly organized, beginning with the
     general principles of child abuse and neglect and lead-
     ing naturally to specific problems. The chapters on the
     developmental aspects, oral and dermatologic manifesta-
     tions of child abuse are useful as it has been diffi-
     cult to find easily accessible literature on these sub-
     jects. In addition, there is a chapter on photography
     of the maltreated child, vitally important for those
     who spend a great deal of time in court.
       Unfortunately only 20 pages of the book are devoted
     to sexual abuse. While the chapter on sexual abuse does
     what it can in the short space available, it can hardly
     be considered adequate at a time when major efforts are
     underway to increase physician awareness of the problem.

134. Felman, Y.M. and J.A. Nikitas. 'Sexually Transmitted
     Diseases and Child Sexual Abuse: I,' *New York State
     Journal of Medicine*, 83 (March 1983) 341-43

Reviews the literature on the epidemiology and diagnosis of child sexual abuse. Problems in identifying the
cause of sexually transmitted diseases in children
include the medical profession's reluctance to suspect
child sexual abuse. Risk factors that lead to such
abuse include adolescent babysitters, crowded household
situations, incestuous families, or highly dysfunctional families who are at greater risk of incest. Signs in
the child that point to sexual abuse include sleeping
difficulties, nightmares and crying out, wanting to re-
locate, eating less, and feeling unsafe. Older children
may show enuresis, hyperactivity, altered sleep patterns, dizzy spells, abdominal pain, compulsive masturbation, or precocious sexual play.

135. Felman, Y.M. and J.A. Nikitas. 'Sexually Transmitted
Diseases and Child Sexual Ausbe: II,' *New York State
Journal of Medicine*, 83 (5) 1983, 714–16
Focuses on the management of pediatric gonococcal infections resulting from sexual abuse. Genital injuries
in children may be subtle but potentially serious if
not recognized. It is further recommended that a
thorough physical examination and history is necessary
for legal documentation of sexual abuse and for proper
medical treatment. Since sexually abused children may
also have been victims of physical abuse.

136. Finkel, K.D. *Recognition and Assessment of the Sexually
Abused Child*. Toronto, Ont.: Ontario Medical Association, 1983 (240 St George St, Toronto, Ont. M5R 2P4)
The purpose of this book is to help physicians understand more fully the nature of childhood sexual abuse,
the significance of the medical examination and the
role of the physician in the assessment of such cases.
A thorough account of childhood sexual abuse involves
consideration of sociomedical, ethical and legal aspects beyond the scope of this document. Physicians who
are likely to be involved in dealing with such cases
would be well advised to read a broader treatise on the
subject. Suggested reading references are listed.

137. Ghent, W.R., DaSylva, N.P. and M.E. Farren. 'Family
Violence: Guides for Recognition and Management,'
*Canadian Medical Association Journal*, 132 (1 March
1985) 541–8

Chronic and intermittent abuse of one family member by another is common. Victims may be children who are sexually or physically abused, wives or live-in partners, or older relatives. Physicians are often the first points of contact for patients who have been abused, but the abuse is frequently concealed by the victims. Physicians should be alert to signs of battering such as bruises in various stages of healing, unusual behaviour in children and interpersonal difficulties in the family. There are a number of options in prevention and treatment, including referral to social service and legal authorities, calling on other resources in the family and helping the individual develop coping skills. This review also lists a large number of social agencies in Canada that are willing to help victims of abuse.

138. Gorline, L.L. 'The Nurse and the Sexually Assaulted Child,' *Current Practice in Pediatric Nursing*, 3 (1980) 155-76
Methods of assisting the sexually abused child through a physical examination and followup are presented, based on the experiences of nurses at the Rape Crisis Program of Memphis, Tennessee. Approximately 25 per cent of the victims seen in the programme are under 14 years of age.

139. Groothuis, J.R., Bischoft, M.C. and L.E. Jaurequi. 'Pharyngeal Gonorrhea in Young Children,' *Pediatric Infectious Disease*, 2 (March 1983) 99-101
A one-year retrospective survey of the medical records of all children seen at a pediatric clinic was undertaken to examine the prevalence of pharyngeal gonorrhea in a population of sexually abused children. All sexually and physically abused children were evaluated using the technique of Farrell et al.

140. Herbert, C.P. 'Sexual Abuse of Children,' *Canadian Family Physician*, 28 (June 1982) 1173-8
Increasing emphasis is being placed on the identification and management of sexual abuse in children. Family physicians have a role to play in identifying and treating these children. Some common myths about sexual abuse are that assaults are made mostly by strangers, that sexual abuse is rare, and that there's nothing

wrong with sex between adults and children. Indicators in the child may be physical or behavioral. In the family, indicators include fathers with low self-esteem, poor relationships with wives, tendency to be domineering and restrictive, and mothers who are passive. Immediate and longterm intervention includes legal, protective and treatment components. The essential factors in successful intervention are belief in the child's disclosure; communication of that belief to the child; and immediate protection of the child and siblings.

141. Maurice, W., Parfitt, K. and L. Maurice. 'Sexual Abuse of Children: Questions and Answers,' *B.C. Medical Journal*, 25 (Jan. 1983) 23-5
Recognizing that treatment facilities for sexual abuse are inadequate in British Columbia, this article answers questions that confront physicians in dealing with the sexual abuse of children. In dealing with the various problems on many levels, created by sexual abuse, the authors propose that physician-groups promote the establishment of comprehensive medically-based treatment resources in B.C.

142. Mega, L.T. and R.E. Cuenca. 'Incest and Physician Responsibility,' *Southern Medical Journal*, 77 (9) 1984, 1109-14
To help physicians take appropriate action with cases of sexual abuse.

143. Woodling, B.A. and P.D. Kossoris. 'Sexual Misuse: Rape, Molestation, and Incest,' *Pediatric Clinics of North America*, 28 (May 1981) 481-99
The discussion serves several purposes to acquaint physicians who may encounter victims of sexual assault with the unique medical problems of sexual assault; to help physicians gain insight into understanding sexual misuse; and to assist in preparing a medicolegal assessment of the problem treating the patient-victim, and testifying in court. Indeed, victims of sexual abuse are special patients who must be treated as such. Insensitivity by the examining physician will adversely affect the patient-victim's physical and emotional welfare.

139   Annotated Bibliography

Mentally Retarded and Sexual Abuse

144. Melberg, K. 'Sexual Abuse of Persons who are Mentally
     Retarded,' *SAMR Dialect*, April, June, Aug. 1984
     (Saskatchewan Association for the Mentally Retarded,
     3031 Louise St., Saskatoon, Sask. S7J 3L1)
     A three-part article which discusses sexual abuse of
     mentally retarded persons in Canada.

Mother-Son Sexuality

145. Janus, S. *The Death of Innocence*. New York, N.Y.:
     William Morrow, 1981
     What is particularly interesting about this book are
     the case histories of mother-son sexuality. This rarely
     takes the form of consummated sexual relations, but in-
     volves various forms of diversion such as bathing of
     the son into adolescence. The boys in these case
     studies found the experience cloying and hateful, but
     were usually able to shake themselves free. The human
     spirit can survive and grow past a variety of seemingly
     stressful experiences. Therapy needs to tap this homeo-
     static drive toward normality which so many human
     beings possess.

146. Shengold, L. 'Some Reflections on a Case of Mother/
     Adolescent Son Incest,' *International Journal of
     Psycho-Analysis*, 61 (Nov. 1980) 475-6
     Begins with a review of Freud's evolving perspective on
     the incest taboo and Oedipal complex. Reviews a case
     history of mother-son incest and discusses the nature
     of the incest barrier and the fear of impregnation by
     the son.

Newsletters

147. National Clearinghouse on Family Violence. *Vis a vis*.
     Ottawa, Ont.: 1985 (Health and Welfare, Ottawa, Ont.
     K1A 1B5)
     A newsletter related to family violence including
     sexual abuse.

148. Ontario Centre for the Prevention of Child Abuse. News-
     letter, Vol 1 No 1, December 1984 (iss. reg. in 1985)

This newsletter contains information about the work of
the Centre, and includes resource materials.

149. Social Planning and Research, United Way of the Lower
Mainland. *Child Sexual Abuse Newsletter*. Vancouver,
B.C.: 1983-5
A newsletter which reports various aspects of sexual
abuse of children in Canadian society. It includes
reviews of new publications and materials.

Overview on Sexual Abuse: Articles

150. Babin, M. and D. Millen. 'The Trauma of Family Sexual
Abuse - Helping the Young Victim,' *Journal*, 26 (March
1982) 1-4 (Ontario Association of Children's Aid
Societies, 2323 Yonge St., Toronto, Ont. M4P 2C9)
Recognition of sexual molestation especially in a family context, can be entirely dependent on the investigating individual's emotional willingness to entertain
the possibility that such abuse does exist.  Such
crimes are difficult to investigate and prosecute
as verification of an allegation is not easy, especially in the absence of physical trauma, or corroborative adult witnesses. The failure to recognize a
child's fabrications as such can subject the family to
unnecessary and troublesome legal action. On the other
hand, failure to recognize the reasons for a victim's
retraction of previous allegations can leave her in
danger of further abuse.

151. Bagley, C. 'Mental Health and the In-Family Sexual
Abuse of Children and Adolescents,' *Canada's Mental
Health*, 32 (June 1984) 17-23
The author addresses basic issues in the sexual abuse
of children within the family. Sexual abuse is distinguished from incest. The cultural roots of sexual abuse
are discussed, and insights of the feminist model are
applied. Various limited studies of incidence and prevalence are reviewed with a view to estimating possible
rates of abuse in Canada. Studies linking early sexual
abuse with a range of serious physical and psychosocial
sequelae are reviewed. The author discusses treatment
models and the goals of treatment, and argues strongly
for improved services to the affected population, and
for a fundamental value change in society that will
eliminate the sexual victimization of children.

152. Chandler, S.M. 'Knowns and Unknowns in Sexual Abuse of
     Children,' *Journal of Social Work and Human Sexuality*,
     1 (Fall-Winter 1982) 51-68
     The knowledge base in many areas of social work prac-
     tice is still fragmented, sometimes unreliable, and of-
     ten contains contradictory 'findings.' The literature
     on the sexual abuse of children is still a potpourri of
     untested theories, poorly designed studies, single-case
     insights, and a research tradition based on small clin-
     ical samples, making generalizations difficult and re-
     sulting in a weak knowledge base for social work prac-
     tice. This paper attempts to help social work practi-
     tioners consider the major findings of the current re-
     search on the sexual abuse of children.

153. Conte, J.R. 'Sexual Abuse of Children: Enduring Issues
     for Social Work,' *Journal of Social Work and Human
     Sexuality*, 1 (Fall-Winter 1982) 1-20
     There may be no other subject matter which instills as
     heated an argument among mental health and social ser-
     vice personnel as that of sexual abuse of children.
     There are a variety of reasons for the frequent polemic
     nature of this argument, including the number of myths
     surrounding sexual abuse of children; the traditional
     disagreements among professionals of different theoret-
     ical models about etiology and treatment; a general
     lack of knowledge concerning most aspects of the prob-
     lem; and the sensitivity of matters dealing with sex-
     uality, especially deviant sexuality and children.
     While this article will not resolve these concerns, it
     is hoped that it will be successful in reviewing a num-
     ber of enduring issues. The issues appear to be endur-
     ing in that they continually are raised and continue to
     affect the services provided sexually abused children
     and the adults who influence and share their lives.
     Some resolution of these issues, at least at the prac-
     tice level, seems necessary if we are to move forward
     on behalf of sexually abused children.

154. Gochros, H.L. 'Social Work and the Sexual Oppression of
     Youth,' *Journal of Social Work and Human Sexuality*, 1
     (Fall-Winter 1982) 37-50
     There no longer seems to be much question as to whether
     social workers *should* be involved with sex-related
     problems; social workers *are* involved. The more perti-
     nent questions today are: are social workers attending

to the most appropriate sex-related problems in the
context of our profession's purposes and values, are
they attacking the most appropriate targets and are
they effective in dealing with these problems?

155. Gordon, S. 'Any Messages for the Child Molester? ...
The Rapist,' *Impact '85*, 1, 4 (Ed-U Press, P.O. Box
583, Fayettville, N.Y. 13066)
A plea to consider the sexual component of molestation
and rape.

156. Gruber, K.J. 'The Child Victim's Role in Sexual Assault
by Adults,' *Child Welfare*, 60 (May 1981) 305-11
Although children are sometimes accused of complying
with adults' demands for sexual relationships, emotional and situational factors force them to become willing victims. Understanding these factors is a better
treatment approach than assigning blame.

157. Herjanic, B. and D. Bryan. 'Quiz: Sexual Abuse of
Children,' *Medical Aspects of Human Sexuality*, 14
(April 1980) 18-20
A quiz dealing with sexual abuse of children.

158. Hyde, N. 'Long-term effects of childhood sexual abuse,'
*British Columbia Medical Journal*, 26 (July 1984) 3-6
Research now is beginning to confirm the long-term
sequalae of the adult incest survivor population who
live with physical effects, sexual dysfunction and
psychosocial effects from their incestuous experiences. The author looks at these three main areas so
that health professionals will recognize symptoms and
symptom complexes that lead to a hypothesis of incest
as a root or contributing cause of the difficulties
being presented by the patient.

159. Kaplan, S.J. and D. Pelcovitz. 'Child Abuse and Neglect
and Sexual Abuse,' *Psychiatric Clinics of North
America*, 5 (Aug. 1982) 321-32
Discusses the definition, incidence, and etiology of
child abuse and explores the characteristics of the
abusing parent and the abused child. An examination of
the environmental factors that play a role in abuse,
such as examination of the environmental factors that
play a role in abuse, such as stress and social

isolation, is followed by a review of effective treatment programmes. It is maintained that a multidisciplinary treatment team needs to aim interventions at
variables operating at all levels of the problem: individual psychopathology, family dysfunction, stress, and
lack of social supports. Hospital management of child
abuse and neglect is also addressed.

160. Mrazek, P.B. 'Sexual Abuse of Children,' *Journal of
Child Psychology and Psychiatry and Allied Disciplines*,
Vol 21, No 1 (1980) 91-5
The incidence and etiology of sexual abuse of children
in the United States is briefly examined, along with
comments on recognition, intervention, outcome, and
prognosis. Reports of such offenses have increased
dramatically in recent years due to legislation and
public awareness campaigns and the probable reasons for
abuse are associated with socioeconomic factors, over-
crowding, social isolation, subcultural values, psychopathology in the perpetrator and/or child, alcoholism,
and family discord, personality disorder, and emotional
deprivation. Physicians and mental health professionals
faced with abuse cases should support treatment for
both child and family which focuses on alleviation of
the root cause. It is noted that outcome and prognosis
data from current treatment programmes are scarce.

161. Rubinelli, J. 'Incest: It's Time We Face Reality,'
*Journal of Psychiatric Nursing and Mental Health
Services*, 18 (April 1980) 17-18
The devastating effects of incest, and the secrecy with
which incidents are treated, demand that the problem
receive immediate attention. Sexually abused children
are robbed of their develomentally determined control
over their bodies and often made to feel responsible.
Long-range effects of incest include depression, sexual
dysfunction, loss of self-esteem, suicidal tendencies,
and psychosis. Though the data supporting these generalizations were taken from cases in which female children were the victims, evidence indicates that male
victims, who are less likely to be identified as incest
victims, suffer similar or more serious problems.

162. Schlesinger, B. 'Sexual Abuse of Children: Knowns and Unknowns,' *Conciliation Courts Review*, 21 (Dec. 1983) 71-80

A review of the literature on sexual abuse of children up to 1982.

163. Star, B. 'Patterns in Family Violence,' *Social Casework*, 61 (June 1980) 339-46
The prevalence of physical and sexual abuse among family members is greater than most people realize. A generic approach to the study of abuse in families suggests that there are many similarities among assaulter characteristics, victim characteristics, and the family interactions that underlie all forms of family violence.

164. Stechler, G. 'Facing the Problem of the Sexually Abused Child,' *New England Journal of Medicine*, 301 (7 Feb. 1980) 348-9
A brief overview of sexual child abuse is presented. Because it involves violation of strong taboos (sex with children, incest, and forced sex), sexual abuse may invoke strong feelings and harsh judgments which may interfere in the care of the abused child and his family if not adequately controlled and understood. Characteristics of offenders are diverse, and a relationship can be discerned between socially condoned, developmentally necessary affectional behaviour and that which is condemned and damaging. For the clinician, the sequence or events can be viewed as occurring in four phases: the actual sexual encounter, the events leading to the child's concealing or revealing the events; the child's attempt to make the event public; and acute and emergency care and followup. The importance of care and support for the less obvious and more enduring aspects of the trauma of sexual abuse is emphasized.

165. *Tellus*. 'Special Issue on Sexual Abuse of Children.' Ottawa, Ont.: Planned Parenthood Federation of Canada, Vol 5 (Winter 1984) (200 151 Slater St., Ottawa, Ont. K1P 5H3)
Contains three articles related to sexual abuse of children.

Overview on Sexual Abuse: Books and Booklets

166. Armstrong, L. *The Home Front: Notes from the Family War Zone*. New York, N.Y.: McGraw-Hill, 1983

Using well-documented and well-researched evidence,
Armstrong outlines the history of family violence in
compelling human terms. She describes the many ways
American lawyers, psychologists, and social workers
have unsuccessfully tried to 'cure' it. Armstrong suggests that those truly concerned with preserving 'the
family' as a credible institution deserving of commit-
ment and trust, must support fundamental constitutional
protections for those seriously victimized within its
borders.

167.  Constantine, L. and F. Martinson, eds. *Children and
Sex: New Findings, New Perspectives.* Boston: Little,
Brown, 1981
David Finkelhor contributes a chapter on his work on
sibling incest, which is the only type of incest which
does not seem to have, for the typical child participant, long term adverse consequences. However, where
siblings were several years separate in age, and when
an older brother coerced a much younger sister into
sexual relations, psychological outcomes were as adverse as in father-daughter incest. Finkelhor's important research findings suggest a profile of the children most vulnerable to sexual assault by a related
adult. Girls most at risk are aged between 10 and 12,
in a lower-income family in a rural area, where either
mother had been absent for periods of time, or a stepfather was present. The amount of long-term trauma is
related to the age of the aggressor (adult males caused
the most trauma), the degree of force and threat to coerce the victim into compliant silence, the length of
time over which the assaults took place, the carry
through of the assaults from pre- to post-adolescence,
and the degree of consummation of the sexual relationship.

168.  Finkelhor, D. *Child Sexual Abuse: New Theory and
Research.* New York, N.Y.: The Free Press, 1984
Initital chapters deal with aspects of abuse that have
previously suffered from neglect or misunderstanding:
the evolution of abuse as a social problem; the precise
moral issues of sex between adults and children; the
characteristics of high-risk children and of perpetrators; and, of special note, the critical preconditions
for sexual abuse to take place. The remainder of the
book discusses new data gathered from recent field

studies showing the prevalence of child sexual abuse today; the extent of public knowledge of abuse; what parents tell children about sexual abuse; the degree to which boys are victims; the degree to which women are abusers; long-term effects of childhood sexual abuse; and the serious problems that continue to hamper social service delivery. Finkelhor concludes by synthesizing his findings and themes and developing their implications for future theory, research, and practice.

169. Fortune, M.M. *Sexual Violence: The Unmentionable Sin.* New York, N.Y.: Pilgrim Press, 1983
This monograph examines the social and religious roots of sexual violence.

170. Gabarino, J. and G. Gillian. *Understanding Abusive Families.* Toronto, Ont.: Lexington Books, 1980
This book constitutes an up-to-date reliable source of descriptive research findings and treatment approaches on the topics of physical, emotional and sexual abuse of infants, children and adolescents. As well, the sections on social isolation and parental roles are very complete and enlightening.

171. Giarretto, H. *Integrated Treatment of Child Sexual Abuse: A Treatment and Training Manual.* Pal Alto, Calif.: Science and Behavior Books, Inc., 1982
Giarretto's method for healing families in which a child has been damaged by incest or sexual assault by a family member is based on two principles for counsellor training: a person cannot become an effective counsellor or indeed a worthwhile human being without first attending diligently to his or her own self-realization; and a person's self-realization cannot be sought successfully if she does not continually strive for social conditions that foster the self-realization of others. These principles are based on the work of Chaudhuri and Maslow, and are distilled into a final overriding idea. A person's strongest drive is to feel good about himself and about others. Only when humans feel good do they value themselves and others and develop nurturing relationships.

172. Halliday, L. *The Silent Scream: The Reality of Sexual Abuse.* Campbell River, B.C.: Linda Halliday, 1982
(R.R. #1, Campbill River, B.C. V9W 3S4)

From the Preface: 'In setting up the self help group
for sexual abuse victims and writing this book, my aim
is to show other victims that there is hope for a full
and productive life if they want it and to encourage
other communities, regardless of size, that they can
provide a program to combat sexual abuse and the problems surrounding it by a joint community effort.
  By sharing my story with others it is my hope that
they will come to understand instead of judge those of
us who have been victimized. In this way sexual abuse
victims will have some input into programs and laws to
help the victims and their families. I am hopeful that
this program will help eliminate the isolation and deg-
radation and provide a contact point, a beginning, for
those who want and need it. This type of group support
could cut down the years of hopeless misery and self
destruction that becomes a part of so many victims.'

173. Kempe, R.S. and C.H. Kempe. *The Common Secret: Sexual
Abuse of Children and Adolescents*. New York, N.Y.:
W.H. Freeman, 1984
The authors go beyond the statistics to include a number of case studies, most drawn from their own patient
list. They take an insightful look at the various forms
of sexual child abuse, from pedophilia and exhibition-
ism to rape and child pornography, and allay many of
the myths which have hindered a fair appraisal of the
problem's severity during the past 25 years. The appendix details the Incest Diversion Program, which has
successfully minimized the number of criminal filings
on incestuous fathers in several states.

174. Metropolitan Toronto Police. *Sexual Abuse*. Toronto,
Ont.: 1983
This booklet deals with the sexual abuse of children.
It is geared to the average citizen.

175. Mrazek, P.B. and C.H. Kempe, eds. *Sexually Abused
Children and Their Families*. New York, N.Y.: Pergamon
Press, 1981
The definition and recognition of child sexual abuse
present many problems. Personal and professional values
and ideologies of those who are concerned about this
social problem often makes consensual agreement regarding its nature difficult. Chapters one and two by the
Mrazeks help to establish a frame of reference and a

shared theoretical basis for the readers. Chapter one
points to the attitudinal changes regarding adult-child
sexual relations throughout time and across cultures. A
diversity of definitions is offered to the reader and
current problems in recognizing sexual abuse cases are
explored. In chapter two the psychosexual development
of the individual and the life cycle of the family system are reviewed. Using this framework, a conceptualization of the psychosexual development of the family
is put forward which emphasizes the critical nature of
the 'mesh' between the child's and parents' personal
psychosexual issues. Sexual abuse of a child can then
be seen as an extreme dysfucntion, representing the
pathological end of a continuum of sexual experience.
Anna Freud, in chapter three, discusses the complex
relationship between the sexual abuse and a child's own
secret wishes which normally remain in the realm of
fantasy. Using the United Kingdom as an example of how
difficult the recognition process can be, Mrazek,
Lynch, and Bentovim in chapter four present the results
of a large survey they conducted while all three authors were living in England. The United Kingdom is not
unique in its reluctance to acknowledge that sexual
abuse of children is a serious problem; rather, social
denial and avoidance appear to be the usual case and
represent early stages in the national recognition process.

176. Pressman, B. *Family Violence: Origins and Treatment*.
Guelph, Ont.: Office for Educational Practice,
University of Guelph, 1984 (Raithby House, University
of Guelph, Guelph, Ont. N1G 2W1)
This authoritative Canadian work on family violence
represents a unique blend of theory and practice. The
concepts are well-conceived in view of current theories. Based on the author's solid understanding and
application of family systemic theory, the book is
prescriptive and instructive.

177. Rush, F. *The Best Kept Secret: Sexual Abuse of
Children*. Englewood Cliffs, N.J.: Prentice-Hall, 1980
In this study of child molestation, Florence Rush, a
psychiatric social worker, reveals the historical
patterns which have been instrumental in sanctioning

and perpetuating child/adult sex through the ages.
Discussing such practices as Greek 'Boy Love,' the
Victorian 'cult of the little girl,' and international
child prostitution, the author exposes the many social
modes, religious interpretations and Freudian cover-ups
fostered by a societal double standard which crosses
all social, economic and racial lines. She further
demonstrates how certain unconscious elements buried
deep in the male psyche have allowed sex between adult
males and juvenile females to escape the disapproval it
deserves.

178. Russell, D.E.H. *Sexual Exploitation: Rape, Child Sexual
Abuse, and Workplace Harassment.* Beverly Hills,
Calif.: Sage, 1984
Who are the perpetrators of sexual assault? Who are the
victims? Russell sheds new light on the prevalence and
causes of three forms of sexual exploitation - rape,
child sexual abuse, and sexual harassment in the workplace. Within a useful analytical framework, she inte-
grates extensive literature on these topics, revealing
numerous links between issues that are often considered
separate and distinct. Her ground-breaking random
sample survey of the experiences of 930 women in San
Francisco adds further insights.

179. Sanford, T.L. *The Silent Children.* New York, N.Y.:
Anchor Press, 1980
The purpose of this book is to examine and understand
the crime of child sexual abuse. With a working knowledge of the circumstances of child molestation and incest, and insight into the motivations of the offenders, parents will be able to translate this information
into positive warnings to their children. Sanford shows
them how to adapt their instruction to the child's age
and to the values and life-style of their family.
    Parents are advised to make their children feel good
about themselves; to avoid making children vulnerable
by sex role stereotyping; to make children understand
just how much other people can physically and emotionally ask from them; and to teach the children the ultimate lesson in prevention; to trust their instincts and
act in their own best interests.

180. Schlesinger, B. *Sexual Abuse of Children: A Resource Guide and Annotated Bibliography*. Toronto, Ont.: University of Toronto Press, 1982
This selective guide is the first North American resource to gather together diverse information on sexual abuse including findings about incest, non-family abuse, the offender, legal aspects of sexual offences, and the treatment of the abused. Also included are a recommended basic library on the subject and a list of available films.
Designed for educators and students alike in faculties of education, medicine, nursing, and social work, it will be most useful for in-service training courses in health and welfare institutions and community college courses for para-professionals.
There are 180 annotations up to 1980.

181. Schultz, G., ed. *The Sexual Victimology of Youth*. Springfield, Ill.: Charles C. Thomas, 1980
This book of readings, presents a series of articles which examine the problems, diagnoses, and treatment of sexual abuse of youth. The inaccurate and insensitive stereotyping that often accompanies this subject has been avoided and realistic intervention methods are presented. This straightforward compendium will be a useful reference for social workers, psychiatrists, psychologists, pediatricians, prosecutors, probation officers, and all those practicing in the fields of mental health and child development.

Paedophilia

182. O'Carroll, T. *Paedophilia: The Radical Case*. Boston, Mass.: Alyson, 1983
An exploration of the philosophical, legal and practical questions of paedophilia.

183. Taylor, B., ed. *Perspectives on Paedophilia*. London, Eng.: Batsford Academic, 1981
What is clear from the papers in this book is that lonely, rejected children with poor self-image, and no adult with whom they can have a normal, caring relationship are particularly vulnerable to the paedophile's approach. Other evidence shows too that they are particularly vulnerable, as recruits to the child

pornography and child prostitution industry. Although
an isolated sexual assault not involving rape or intercourse can cause relatively little harm to a child,
this book produces further evidence to show that prolonged coerced sexual contact can have devastating effects on children.

## Personal Experiences

184. Allen, C.V. *Daddy's Girl*. Toronto, Ont.: McClelland &
Stewart, 1980
The author discusses the incestuous abuse she suffered
as a child victim of her father.

185. Olds, S.W. *The Eternal Garden: Seasons of our
Sexuality*. New York, N.Y.: Times Books, 1985
Author's letter: 'I tell the stories of three individuals whom I interviewed whose lives were greatly affected by sexual abuse in their childhoods. I also cite
various research sources on the impact and prevalance
of such abuse.

186. Ricks, C. *Carol's Story*. Wheaton, Ill.: Tyndale House,
1981
Presents the personal narrative of Carol, a victim of
childhood incest. This true story recounts her family
life, the incestuous relationship with her father, and
the emotional and psychological problems she encountered both as a child and as an adult.

187. Smallwood, M. 'Incest – It Happes in the Best of
Families,' *Rochester Women* (Feb. 1985) 28-9 and 32
A personal story about a stepson who molested a 12-
year-old girl.

## Pre-school Children and Sexual Abuse

188. Funk, J.B. 'Management of Sexual Molestation in Pre-
Schoolers,' *Clinical Pediatrics*, 19 (Oct. 1980) 686-8
Guidelines are presented to aid in the management of
single-incident, non-violent sexual exploitation of the
preschool child. Objectives include safeguarding the
child, dealing with any physical trauma and facilitat-
ing a quick resolution for the acute emotional crisis
for the child and the parents.

Prevention

189. Allan, B. 'Preventing Sexual Abuse of Children,'
*Tellus*, 5 (Winter 1984) 9-13 (Planned Parenthood
Federation of Canada, 200 151 Slater St., Ottawa, Ont.
K1P 5H3)
Parents and professionals working with children are be-
coming increasingly aware of child sexual abuse. Spec-
tacular cases appear almost nightly in newspapers and
TV news. Parents, enlightened as to the possible risks
their children face, are looking for ways of protecting
their children.

190. Sohn, H.A. *Prevention of Sexual Abuse of Children*.
Toronto, Ont.: Child Abuse and Family Violence
Prevention Program, Ontario Ministry of Community and
Social Services, 1982 (10pp)
This paper discusses prevention in the area of sexual
abuse of children.

Programs Related to Sexual Abuse

191. Big Brothers of Canada. *Program for the Prevention of
Child Sexual Abuse*. Burlington, Ont.: 1985 (3019
Harvester Rd., Burlington, Ont. L7N 3G4)
An outline of a programme to train staff, parents, and
children in the area of sexual abuse.

192. The Metropolitan Chairman's Special Committee on Child
Abuse. *Child Sexual Abuse Treatment Resource
Directory*. Toronto, Ont.: March 1984
A listing and description of treatment services and
contacts in the Metropolitan Toronto area, prepared for
use by professionals. (55pp)

193. ------. 'Evaluation of the Preventive Education
Program,' prepared by Women Associates Consulting
Incorporated. Toronto, Ont.: March 1984
Evaluation of 1983 pilot programme on personal safety
involving ten elementary schools and 3,900 children.
The programme involves community orientation, a theat-
rical presentation for children and a follow--up class-
room resource kit. (47pp)

194. ------. 'Guidelines for Investigative Interviewing of
     Child Victims of Sexual Abuse,' prepared by Mary
     Wells. Toronto, Ont.: revised May 1984
     Prepared to assist child welfare and police personnel
     responsible for conducting investigations of alleged
     incidents of sexual abuse. Includes practical and
     proven techniques to assist children to tell their
     stories, thus enabling a full and balanced investiga-
     tion. (8pp)

195. ------. 'An Introduction and Summary of Activities
     (1981-1984),' prepared by Lorna Grant. Toronto, Ont.:
     Dec. 1984
     Reviews the development, philosophy, conceptual frame-
     work and activities of the Special Committee in its
     first three years (12pp)

196. ------. 'Approved Guidelines for Child Abuse Investiga-
     tors and School Personnel as to Participation of School
     Boards in the Investigation.' Toronto, Ont.: Sept. 1984
     Endorsed by seven school boards in Metro, the Police
     Department and the three child welfare agencies.
     Designed as an adjunct to the *Child Sexual Abuse Proto-
     col: Guidelines and Procedures for a Coordinated Res-
     ponse to Child Sexual Abuse in Metropolitan Toronto*,
     approved in Nov. 1983. (5pp)

197. ------. 'Summary of Findings: The Child Sexual Abuse
     Protocol Implementation Study,' prepared by Lorna
     Grant. Toronto, Ont.: Feb. 1985
     Summary of study conducted by The Sutcliffe Group
     Incorporated in August and Sept. 1984 to assess the
     initial impact of and extent to which the *Child Sexual
     Abuse Protocol* had been implemented since approval in
     November 1983. (15pp)

198. ------. 'Crisis Support Group Program: Program Statis-
     tics (1 Jan.-31 Dec. 1984), prepared by Karen Katchen.
     Toronto, Ont.: Feb. 1985
     Reporting and analysis of information received regarding
     423 individuals referred to one of five groups aimed at
     provision of support in the crisis period immediately
     following disclosure of child sexual abuse. (10pp)

199. ------. 'An Introduction to the Preventive Education
     Program for Children.' Toronto: revised March 1985
     Brochure describing the programme offered in elementary
     schools within Metropolitan Toronto aimed at prevention
     and early detection of child abuse, particularly sexual
     abuse. Over 30,000 children along with parents, teach-
     ers and local professionals were involved in the pro-
     gramme in 1983–84.

200. ------. *Developing a Comprehensive Response to Child
     Sexual Abuse: A review of developmental activities over
     the past year with recommendations for future action*,
     prepared by Lorna Grant. Toronto: Oct. 1982
     Approved by the Special Committee in Nov. 1982, this
     report reviews activities and needs in the areas of
     investigation, treatment, prevention and training.
     (17pp plus seven appendices)

201. ------. *The Legal Response to Sexual Abuse of Children:
     A review of current procedural and legal practices in
     the child welfare and criminal justice systems*, pre-
     pared by Marion Lane. Toronto: Oct. 1982
     Review commissioned by the Special Committee in an at-
     tempt to capture the experience of children involved in
     legal proceedings as a result of sexual abuse. Findings
     led to the development of *Child Sexual Abuse Protocol*
     as an initial attempt to minimize further trauma to
     child victims. (107pp plus 12 appendices)

202. ------. Child Sexual Abuse Protocol: Guidelines and
     Procedures for a Coordinated Response to Child Sexual
     Abuse in Metropolitan Toronto. Toronto: Nov. 1983
     Developed over nine months and ratified for implementa-
     tion by the key mandated agencies in Metro Toronto res-
     ponsible for the investigation of child sexual abuse,
     this protocol has served as a model for similar initia-
     tives in numerous other communities. (34pp)

203. National Clearinghouse on Family Violence. *Directory of
     Child Abuse Prevention Programs in Canada*. Ottawa,
     Ont.: 1984
     This directory attempts to offer an overview of the
     many and varied approaches to child abuse prevention.
     Programmes in education, mental health, law, medicine,
     self-help and social services from regions across the

country are included, but the entries listed in this
first edition of the directory by no means represent a
comprehensive picture of child abuse prevention in
Canada. Many communities and programmes remain uniden-
tified; many new programmes will become established.
Also, it is hoped that this publication will stimulate
further activities across the country.

204. Ontario Ministry of Community and Social Services. *A
Progress Report*. Toronto, Ont.: Children's Services
Division (June 1980)

205. Ponée, D. 'Information and Social Change: The National
Clearinghouse on Family Violence.' *Canada's Mental
Health*, 32 (June 1984) 16 and 23
The author briefly describes the mandate, origins and
activities of Health and Welfare Canada's National
Clearinghouse on Family Violence, raising the question
of the role and impact of the information provider in
the struggle against a major social problem like family
violence.

Psychiatric Studies

206. Elmslie, G. and A. Rosenfeld. 'Incest reported by children and adolescents hospitalized for severe psychiatric problems' *American Journal of Psychiatry*, 140
(June 1983) 708–11
A study of 65 9–17 year-olds hospitalized for psychiatric problems revealed a history of incest in six of the
16 nonpsychotic female samples. One of 10 psychotic females and three males also had such a history. A comparison of the nonpsychotic females who had a history
of incest and those who had no known history of incest
or sexual abuse showed no specific effects of incest.
Results indicate that social and psychological pathology
serious enough to warrant hospitalization is not a simple
effect of incest itself but is a consequence of severe
family disorganization and the resulting ego impairment.

207. Mrazek, D.A. 'The Child Psychiatric Examination of the
Sexually Abused Child,' *Child Abuse and Neglect*, 4
(1980) 274–84
Considers the consequences of sexual abuse and distin-
guishes between the child psychiatric evaluation given

to a victim of incest and one conducted with a child
assaulted by someone outside the family. Offers suggestions for the diagnostic process and notes the importance of assessing the immediate needs of the victim and how they can be met by social services.

208. Yates, A. 'Children Eroticized by Incest,' *American
Journal of Psychiatry*, 139 (April 1982) 482-5
Observes that child victims of incest are traditionally perceived as passive victims of sexual assault.
In numerous cases the child actively participates in
the incest and exhibits highly erotic and seductive
behaviour. Asserts that the child may use the incest to
express anger or seek nurturance and pleasure where no
other sources are available. Presents case histories of
eroticized children with particular attention to the
reactions of foster parents who deal with the child's
seductive behaviour.

## Reports

209. Appleford, B. 'Badgley Report Summary.' *CPA Highlights*,
7 (April 1985) 6-10 (558 King Edward Ave., Ottawa,
Ont. K1N 7N6)
A response related to the proposed office of the Commissioner, service provision, reporting and research.

210. Badgley, R.F. (chairman) *Sexual Offenses Against
Children: Report of the Committee on Sexual Offences
Against Children and Youth*. Ottawa, Ont.: Canadian
Government Publishing Centre, 1984 (2 vols)
Sexual abuse of children is incredibly widespread in
Canada and – like an iceberg – only a tiny part of it
is above surface and recognized by the authorities or
the public. This was the finding in the recent two-
volume report on three years of research by the feder-
ally appointed Committee on Sexual Offences Against
Children and Youths. 'Known child sexual abuse is a
fraction of its true occurrence,' says the committee.
Most offences are probably not detected. Of those reported, only a proportion result in charges, fewer
still in convictions.
  One of many major studies found that one in four
girls and one in 10 boys – about 1.4 million Canadians
– had been sexually assaulted. A Canadian Human Rights

survey in 1981 of 2,004 persons aged 18 and over found
that 41.2 per cent (48.7 per cent of women and 33.2 per
cent of men) reported previous sexual harassment.
    The committee, which had been asked to determine the
adequacy of laws and their enforcement in protecting
children against sexual abuse, reported badly, 'On the
basis of our findings about some 10,000 cases of sexual
offences against children and youths, our principal
conclusions are that these crimes occur extensively and
that the protection afforded these young victims by the
law and the public services is inadequate.
    The committee recommends the establishment of 'an
Office of the Commissioner reporting directly to the
Office of the Prime Minister.' It becomes apparent that
the commissioner would be initiating and co-ordinating
preventive efforts by all federal, provincial and private childcare agencies in the country, defining sexual
abuse, develoing new laws to deal with child abusers
and developing compensation for child sexual .victims.

211. Canadian Council on Children and Youth. Synopsis of
     Recommendations Drawn from the Report of the Committee
     on Sexual Offenses against Children. Ottawa, Ont.: 1984
     A comprehensive summary of the Badgley Report.

212. Canadian Government Publishing Centre. *Sexual Offences
     against Children in Canada: Summary*. Ottawa, Ont.: 1984
     A concise summary of the findings of the two-volume
     Report (1314pp) of the Badgley Report.

213. Carter, B. 'The Badgley Report: Commentary,' *OAPSW
     Newsmagazine*, 11 (Nov. 1984) 5 and 9 (Ontario Associa-
     tion of Professional Social Workers)
     A critical analysis of the Badgley Report on Sexual
     Offences against Children and Youth (1984).

214. ------. *A Feminist Perspective on 'The Badgley Report,'
     Sexual Offences against Children*. Toronto, Ont.: OISE,
     Occasional Papers in Social Policy Analysis, Dept. of
     Sociology in Education, Paper ç10, 1985 (252 Bloor
     St. W., Toronto, Ont. M5S 1V6)
     This paper analyzes 'The Badgley Report,' *Sexual Of-
     fences against Children*, with a focus on sexism. A
     specific framework is used to examine six separate
     elements in the report: language concepts, questions

posed, interpretations made, policy recommendations and
overall perspective. The paper also addresses those
recommendations put forward by the committee which are
beneficial to both sexes.

215. Clark, L.M.G. 'Boys Will be Boys: Beyond the Badgley
     Report: A Critical View.' Toronto, Ont.: University of
     Toronto, Centre of Criminology, March 1985 (Room 8001,
     130 St. George St., Toronto, Ont. M5S 1A1)
     A paper presented at a symposium.
       There must be changes in many of our institutions,
     and new institutions developed, which will reflect a
     single standard of behaviour for all interpersonal and
     sexual relationships, based on the equality of men and
     women and their equal and shared responsibility for en-
     suring that all children are given the opportunity to
     become fully actualized autonomous adults; but these
     changes cannot be brought about without facing the fact
     that patriarchy has to go and that paternalism must go
     with it.

216. Dawson, R. The Badgley Report: Implications for Child
     Protective Services. *Journal* (Ontario Association of
     Children's Aid Societies), 28 (Nov. 1984) 8–16
     Although the Report concludes that child sexual abuse
     is a 'pervasive tragedy that has damaged the lives of
     tens of thousands of Canadian children and youths,' the
     problem has yet to be accepted by legislative bodies as
     urgent and significant in terms of national priorities.
     The task for child protection services is to ensure,
     through its voice for children, that government under-
     stand that sexual abuse of children in Canada is exten-
     sive, harmful and requires immediate action. Unless
     those most concerned about children respond positively
     to the overall findings and recommendations of the re-
     port, little government initiative can be expected. The
     importance of this Report is that it provides a factual
     basis for demanding prompt and significant efforts to
     improve protection and services for sexually abused
     children. Getting on the 'National Agenda' is our first
     priority. Verifying the findings and refining the
     recommendations of the Report should be an important
     but secondary concern for child protection services.

217. Fraser, P. (chairman) *Pornography and Prostitution in
     Canada: Report of the Special Committee on Pornography*

*and Prostitution*. Ottawa, Ont.: Canadian Government
Publishing Centre, 1985 (2 vols)
This report includes materials on sexual abuse and
incest as it is related to prostitution.

218. Health and Welfare Canada, *Directory of Child Abuse
Prevention Programs in Canada*. Ottawa, Ont.: National
Clearinghouse on Family Violence, 1984
The National Clearinghouse on Family Violence, a programme of the Department of National Health and Welfare
Canada, is responsible for developing and disseminating
materials on child abuse and neglect across Canada. Established in 1982, the Clearinghouse has been gathering
and collating materials useful to programme planners,
policymakers, researchers, front-line workers and the
general public.
   This directory attempts to offer an overview of the
many and varied approaches to child abuse prevention.
Programmes in education, mental health, law, medicine,
self-help and social services from regions across the
country are included, but the entries listed in this
first edition of the directory by no means represent a
comprehensive picture of child abuse prevention in
Canada. Many communities and programmes remain uniden-
tified; many new programmes will become established.
Also, it is hoped that this publication will stimulate
further activities across the country.

219. Levine, B. Sexual Offences against Children and
Youths. Understanding and Action: An Overview of the
Major Findings of the Badgley Report. Toronto, Ont.:
Alliance for Children, Ontario, 1985 (Ste. 401, 234
Eglinton Ave. E., Toronto, Ont. M4P 1K5)
A seven-page summary of the Badgley Report.

220. Macdonald, D. 'Sexual Offenses against Children: The
Badgley Report,' *Current Issue Review*, 84-38E. Ottawa,
Ont.: Library of Parliament, 1985
A short overview of the Badgley Report.

221. National Clearinghouse on Family Violence. *Proceedings
of the National Consultation Day on Child Abuse,
Montreal, September 10, 1984*. Ottawa, Ont.: 1985
The objectives identified by the planning committee
were as follows: 1) exchange between various individuals and groups working in the field of child abuse in

Canada; 2) opportunity for front-line and decision-
making persons to examine the strengths and weaknesses
of the Badgley Report; 3) motivation for action by participants in the form of legislative input, advocacy
and other concrete actions; and 4) identification by
the participants of the most important issues and recommendations arising from the Report. This priorized
list of issues would guide the various departments,
agencies and associations (private and public) in their
medium and long-term planning.

222. Ontario Centre for Prevention of Child Abuse. *Child
Abuse Publications and Reports*. 1984 (700 Bay St.,
Suite 2106, Toronto, Ont. M7A 1E9
A listing of available publications including sexual
abuse of children.

Research Studies

223. Bagley, C. and M. McDonald. 'Adult Mental Health
Sequels of Child Sexual Abuse, Physical Abuse and
Neglect in Maternally Separated Children,' *Canadian
Journal of Community Mental Health*, 3 (Spring 1984)
15-26
A follow-up study is reported of the mental health and
psychosexual adjustment in young adulthood of 57 girls
who were removed from home in childhood by Social
Service agencies because of abuse, neglect or family
breakdown. Twenty of the girls had experienced sexual
abuse within the family context before the age of 14.
The 57 maternally separated girls were compared with 30
girls who had experienced non-disrupted childhood. Multiple regression analysis showed that early sexual
abuse explained more of the variance in adult adjustment than either physical abuse and neglect, or maternal separation. It is concluded that, subject to the
limits of the sample, early sexual abuse within the
family has severe long-term implications for mental
health in adulthood unless appropriate therapeutic intervention is offered. Combinations of sexual abuse
with physical abuse or neglect commenced early in the
child's life, having particularly adverse outcomes.

224. Ballew, J.R. 'Role of Natural Helpers in Preventing
Child Abuse and Neglect,' *Social Work*, 30
(Jan.-Feb. 1985) 37-41

Are families who are considered at risk of abusing or neglecting their children socially isolated, or do they have access to informal helping networks? This article reports the results of a study showing that friends, relatives, and neighbours are potential helpers for such families and are effective in resolving the problems they address. The author investigates the role – which can be mediated by a social worker – of these natural helpers in prevention.

225. Byrne, J.P. and E.V. Valdiserrt. 'Victims of Childhood Sexual Abuse: A Follow-up Study of a Noncompliant Population,' *Hospital & Community Psychiatry*, 33 (Nov. 1982) 938–40
Investigated victims of pediatric sexual assault, paying particular attention to determining the current status of the child, evaluating the family for social and psychological changes, and discovering what factors had interfered with follow-up. Samples were 34 1–14-year-olds who did not return for follow-up after treatment at an emergency room for sexual assault. Results are consistent with previous studies that suggest that victims of childhood sexual abuse are subject to emotional and behavioural sequelae.

226. Boatman, B., Borkan, E.L. and D.H. Schetky. 'Treatment of Child Victims of Incest,' *American Journal of Family Therapy*, 9 (Winter 1981) 43–51
Presents a descriptive review of three treatment methods: individual, group, and family therapy used over a five-year period with 40 3–16 year old child incest victims. Common themes, issues, and pitfalls that arose during therapy are discussed with respect to a damaged sense of self, guilt and anger, sexuality, and countertransference.

227. Cantwell, H.B. 'Sexual abuse of Children in Denver 1979: Reviewed with Implications for Pediatric Intervention and Possible Prevention,' *Child Abuse and Neglect*, 5 (1981) 75–85
Analyzes 287 cases of child sexual abuse investigated by the Denver Department of Social Services in 1979.

228. Finkelhor, D. and G.T. Hotaling. 'Sexual Abuse in the Natonal Incidence Study of Child Abuse and Neglect: An Appraisal,' *Child Abuse and Neglect*, 8 (1), 1984, 47–53

The National Incidence Study of Child Abuse and Neglect was a major, government sponsored effort to collect data on reported and unreported child abuse. It used a systematic representative sample methodology and very precisely developed definitions of child abuse. This paper reviews some of the main limitations of the study in regard to findings on sexual abuse. First, there is probably less 'new' data in the study on sexual abuse than on other forms of abuse, since so many of the study cases of sexual abuse were 'officially reported' cases. In addition, the study limited its definition of sexual abuse only to cases where a caretaker was the perpetrator, a definition that is much more restrictive than what is used in many treatment programmes. Finally, the data on perpetrators has a number of problems that stem from the study's definitions of sexual abuse. This paper makes suggestions for future incidence type studies of sexual abuse.

229. Gilgun, J.F. 'Does the Mother Know? Alternatives to Blaming Mothers for Child Sexual Abuse,' *Response*, 7 (Fall 1984) 2-4
This report is part of a larger study of the sexual abuse of young females. In the larger study, 117 girls and boys aged 10 to 15, who were a volunteer sample from the general population, were surveyed on items thought to be relevant to child sexual abuse. In addition, 20 girls aged 10 to 15 known to have been sexually abused were interviewed an average of five times each. For 17 of these girls, their parents/primary caretakers were interviewed an average of two times each, with a range of two to five. Subjects were recruited for heterogeneity of subjects by type of offense, age of subject, length of victimizing relationship, and race. Information on the role of all family members was collected. Interviewing more than one member of the family and multiple interviews provide cross-validation of findings. Interview data were collected between 1 April 1982 and 20 May 1983.

230. Goodwin, J.M., McCarthy, T. and P. DiVasto. 'Prior Incest in Mothers of Abused Children,' *Child Abuse and Neglect*, 5 (1981) 87-95
Reports the results of a study to determine if mothers of abused children had higher incidences of incest.

Compared to a similar control group, mothers of abused
children did report a significantly higher number of
prior incestuous activities, 24 per cent as opposed to
only three per cent for the control group.

231. Jackson, T.L. and W.P. Ferguson. 'Attribution of blame
in incest,' *American Journal of Community Psychology*,
11 (June 1983) 313-22
This study was designed to identify the empirical
structure of attitudes relating to attribution of blame
in incest. A second purpose was to determine how variables such as gender, physically abused status, and
sexually abused status influence the attribution of
blame in incest. The sample consisted of 201 male and
211 female college students who were administered the
Jackson Incest Blame Scale. Four factors emerged from
the factor analysis of the total sample supporting the
hypothesis that attribution of blame in incest is a
multidimensional construct including victim, offender,
situational, and social factors. A difference in the
level of victim blame was found between male and female
samples. Apparently men blame the victim for her assault more than women.

232. Khan, N. and M. Sexton. 'Sexual Abuse of Young
Children, *Clinical Pediatrics*, 22 (May 1983) 369-72
For an 18-month period, all sexual abuse cases seen at
a university hospital were referred to a project social
worker. Data from the initial interview and medical
records were analyzed for 113 children who were 12
years of age or younger. Half of the cases were five
years or younger and three-fourths of the cases were
female. Reasons why females are more likely to be identified as sexually abused are discussed. A higher-than-
average rate of gonorrhea was found among samples.
While only 44 per cent of abusers were relatives of the
abused, 93 per cent were known to the family.

233. Little-Sorrenti, L., Bagley, C. and S. Robertson. 'An
Operational Definition of the Long-term Harmfulness of
Sexual Relations with Peers and Adults by Young
Children,' *Canadian Children*, 9 (1984) 46-57
Self-report data on sexual abuse during childhood by
568 young adult students (404 women and 164 men) have
been considered in relation to self-concept as adults.

The seriousness of earlier abuse was defined operation-
ally by its significant correlation with poor self-
concept as a young adult. Using this operational cri-
terion, serious sexual abuse involved someone at least
three years older than the victim *or* the use of force
or threat, to achieve a sexual relationship involving
handling or interference with the child's unclothed
genitals, or attempted or achieved intercourse. According to these operational definitions, nineteen per cent
of females in this college sample suffered serious sexual abuse by the time they were sixteen. By definition,
this 19 per cent had significantly poorer self-concept
than those who had not been abused.

234. Martin, M.J. and J. Walters. 'Familial Correlates of
Selected Types of Child Abuse and Neglect,' *Journal of
Marriage and the Family*, 44 (May 1982) 267-76
The study, based on 489 cases of child abuse and neglect, was designed to determine specific patterns of
family circumstance which tended to be present in families in which: 1) abandonment; 2) physical abuse; 3)
emotional abuse; 4) neglect; or 5) sexual abuse had
been substantiated. Although previous studies have
tended to treat child abuse and neglect as a unidimen-
sional dependent variable, the findings of this investigation indicate that different kinds of abuse are related to different antecedent variables and suggest
that the patterns are complex.

235. Paretti, P.O. and D. Banks. 'Negative Psychological
Effects on the Incestuous Daughter of Sexual Relations
with her Father,' *Panminerva Medica*, 22 (March 1980)
27-30
A study of 41 women, ranging in age from 15 to 23
years, who had had incestuous relationships with their
fathers was designed to examine the negative psychosocial vari-ables operating in father-daughter incest.
Resistance and involuntary participation were marked as
constant variables. All subjects had received counseling at Catholic churches in Chicago, Illinois. Participation in incest ranged from 10 months to seven years
with a mean of 2.3 years.

236. Scherzer, L.N. and L. Padma. 'Sexual Offenses Committed
against Children,' *Clinical Pediatrics*, 19 (Oct. 1980)
679-85

A descriptive analysis was done on 73 consecutive cases
of childhood sexual abuse seen in 1978. There were conspicuous similarities among the cases. Sexually abused
children tended to come from households with evidence
of family stress. The events occurred in safe havens
such as the children's own homes, by individuals known
and trusted by the children. An intrafamilial stress-
dysfunction model, rather than a victim-assailant
model, is more applicable to childhood sexual abuse.

237. Tsai, M. and M.N. Wagner. 'Incest and Molestation:
Problems of Childhood Sexuality,' *Medical Times*, 109
(July 1981) 16-19
This brief description of a study performed at the
University of Washington focuses on the relationship
between the incest victim and the offender, characteristics of victims and offenders, effects of the crime,
and the role of the family physician in educating and
helping the victim. The study, which involved 118 women
sexually molested as children, revealed that the father
was the molester in 26.3 per cent of the cases, the
stepfather in 15.2 per cent, a neighbour or acquaint-
ance in 12.7 per cent, a family friend in 11 per cent,
and the grandfather in 10.2 per cent.

238. Tucker-Adams, C. 'A Sociological Overview of 28 Sex-
Abused Children,' *Child Abuse and Neglect*, 5 (1981)
361-7
A retrospective overview of 28 sexually-abused children
evaluated at a university-based child guidance clinic
is reported. These 28 cases are scrutinized and empirical data are culled on the following socio-demographic
and clinical variables: age, gender, race, family com-
position, referral source, presenting complaints, type
of referral, psychiatric history of the child and
family, diagnosis, disposition, type and duration of
treatment, and a severity rating (done by parents) of
the child's behavioural maladjustment. Historical information about the sexual abuse is presented: molester, type
of abuse, duration of abuse and recency of sex abuse.

239. West, D.J., ed. *Sexual Victimisation: Two Recent
Researches into Sex Problems and their Social Effects*.
Brookfield, Vt.: Gower, 1985
This book presents the results of two studies – the
first of girl victims of sexual molestation, and the

second of social victimization of homosexual males.
Amongst other findings, the research reveals a much
higher incidence of expeiences of sexual abuse, than
the relatively few cases tht come before the courts
would lead one to expect and a prevalence of discrim-
ination in spite of a generally improved climate of
tolerance.

240. de Young, M. *The Sexual Victimization of Children*.
Jefferson, N.C.: McFarland and Co., 1982
In this study incest is defined as sexual intercourse,
attempted sexual intercourse, or sexual contact of
either a heterosexual or a homosexual nature between
people too closely related to legally marry. In order
to study incest, a large clinical sample composed of
incest victims, offenders, and nonparticipating family
members was created.
   Eighty victims of incest are part of that large clinical sample. At the time of the study they ranged in
age from four to 53 years, with a mean age at the time
of the study of 23 years. Eight (10%) of those 80 victims are males. Obviously that wide age range means
that some of the victims were just emerging from their
incest experience at the time of the study while others
were retrospectively describing their experiences.

241. ------. 'Self-Injurious Behavior in Incest Victims: A
Research Note,' *Child Welfare*, 61 (Nov.-Dec. 1982) 577-84
Self-injurious behaviour has only recently been recognized as a behavioural manifestation of physically battered children. The author reports a high rate of that
behaviour in sexually abused children and proposes a
number of etiological factors accounting for it.

Review of the Literature

242. Bagley, C. 'Childhood Sexuality and the Sexual Abuse of
Children: A Review of the Monograph Literature 1978 to
1982,' *Journal of Child Care*, 1 (3) 1983, 105-27
A comprehensive review of books related to child sexual
abuse during the 1978-82 period.

243. ------. 'Child Sexual Abuse: A Bibliography of Journal
Studies 1978-1982,' *Journal of Child Care*, 1 (5) 1983,
81-86

A review of journal articles on sexual abuse of
children during the 1978–82 period.

244. Freund, K., Heasman, G.A. and V. Roper. 'Results of
the main studies on sexual offences against children
and pubescents (a review),' *Canadian Journal of
Criminology*, 24 (Oct. 1982) 387–97
A literature review focused on seventy-four studies of
father-daughter incest and nonincestuous sexual offenses against young children and preadolescents. Epidemiological and demographic studies were the most in-
formative, although few were exhaustive. These studies
were limited to data primarily gathered for purposes
other than the assessment of sexual offenses against
children and therefore were not satisfactory. The remaining studies used small samples and were conducted
under severe financial restraint. Findings that warrant
more stringent research methods relate to 1) the difference in the recidivism rate noted in heterosexual
and homosexual offenders against children, which indicated that heterosexual offenders are not pedophiles;
2) the large proportion of male offenders who were ex-
hibitionists; 3) the difference between heterosexual
and homosexual offenders against children with respect
to their childhood relationships with their own
fathers; and 4) the three-peaked age distribution of
nonexhibitionist sex offenders against children and
preadolescents.

245. Frude, N. 'The Sexual Nature of Sexual Abuse,' *Child
Abuse and Neglect*, 6 (1982) 211–23
The growing literature on sexual abuse within the
family is reviewed within the context of a simple model
which emphasizes the role of sexual factors and it de-
emphasizes some of the 'dynamic' factors which many
other authors have stressed. Evidence from a number of
studies is quoted and found to support the view that
fathers engaging in sexual activity with their daughters often have unfilled sexual needs.

246. Koch, M. 'Sexual Abuse of Children,' *Adolescence*, 15
(Fall 1980) 643–8
A review of recent English language literature dealing
with the sexual abuse of children.

247. Luther, L. and J.H. Price. 'Child Sexual Abuse: A
Review,' *The Journal of School Health*, 50 (March 1980)
161-5
The sexual abuse of children is a significant problem
in the United States. It is a traditionally touchy
subject which has been hidden by cultural stereotypes
and taboos. It is only in the last ten, and especially
the last five years that the true scope and essence of
child sexual abuse has begun to be understood. This article reviews the recent literature dealing with child
sexual abuse and identifies the role health educators
can play in combatting this problem. There were 35
items in the bibliography.

248. Lystad, M.H. 'Sexual Abuse in the Home: A Review of the
Literature,'*International Journal of Family Psychiatry*,
3 (1) 1982, 3-31
Reviews theoretical, incidence, and causal studies of
sexual abuse in the home. Research has focused primarily on father-daughter abuse; other kinds of abuse -
marital rape, sexual abuse between father and son or
between mother and son, abuse of children by step-
parents, abuse of parents by sexual partners, and abuse
among siblings - have received relatively little attention. Research has focused on the social and psychological characteristics of the victim, offender, and
other family members who collude in the crime by ignor-
ing it or encouraging its occurrence. The problem is
seen primarily as one of family dysfunction, although
it may be accompanied by psychiatric disorder. It is
more likely to occur in families where warm, caring
feeling and responsibilities toward family members are
absent and where social status among members is diver-
gent so that the more powerful easily use force over
the less powerful. The latter generally accept the assault because of cultural norms. To a lesser extent,
such abuse is more likely to occur when victims and/or
offenders have neurological deficiencies. The lack of
data on incidence is a serious disadvantage in understanding the problem and in educating the public about
its severity and the need for intervention and prevention services. Some prevention strategies gleaned from
the limited research that has been done are presented.
(113 references)

249. Mey Vander, B.J. and R.L. Neff. 'Adult-Child Incest: A
     Review of Research and Treatment,' *Adolescence*, 17
     (Winter 1982) 717-33
     Twenty-six independent studies are examined in this re-
     view and related treatment and theoretical literature
     is also discussed.

250. Price, J.M. and E.V. Valdiserri. 'Childhood Sexual
     Abuse: A Recent Review of the Literature,' *Journal of
     the American Medical Women's Association*, 36 (July
     1981) 232-4
     Analyzes the recent literature on child sexual abuse.
     Virtually all published studies show an increase in
     cases but note that many cases, especially those in-
     volving incest, are not reported. Difficulties in the
     detection of incestuous child abuse are frequently
     noted and recommendations identified.

251. Simari, C.G. and D. Baskin. 'Incest: No Longer a Family
     Affair,' *Child Psychiatry Quarterly*, 13 (April-June
     1980) 36-51
     Reviews the literature on incest. All aspects of the
     topic, from detection to treatment, are included. Ef-
     fects on an incest victim are described using the ex-
     ample of a thirty-five-year-old woman.

252. Speert-Lawton, S. and A. Wachtel. *Child Sexual Abuse in
     the Family: A Review of Trends in the Literature and
     the Incest Taboo: Some Theories*. Vancouver, B.C.:
     United Way of the Lower Mainland, 1982
     This paper reviews changes in the analysis of child
     sexual abuse from the early decades of the century to
     the present. The most striking of these changes were:
     1) initially, incest was seen as an uncommon and atypi-
     cal form of child sexual abuse. That perception has
     changed to the extent that much current theorizing
     about the causes and dynamics of child sexual abuse
     centre on abuse within the family setting; and 2) a
     long period of interest in trying to characterize the
     particular deviant nature of the abuser has given way
     to a strong focus on family dynamics and the 'dysfunc-
     tional family.'
        The bulk of theorizing has focussed on father-
     daughter incest. Other incestuous relationships have

been somewhat neglected. All the same, the literature
on father-daughter incest does promise new insights
into the factors underlying the general problem of
child sexual abuse.

## Rural Settings and Sexual Abuse

253. Sigurdson, E. and K. Jones. 'The Development of a Rural
Team to Deal with Child Abuse,' *Canadian Family
Physician*, 28 (June 1982) 1180-4
In the last ten years teams for dealing with child
abuse have become established in many urban centres.
More recently rural communities have started similar
programmes; such a team was established in rural
Manitoba in 1976. A series of events since then has
improved the operation of the team. Cooperation with an
urban team has enhanced the functioning of the rural
team. A broad base of community support for this work
has been essential. A review of cases seen in the last
18 months indicates 12 cases are physical abuse, nine
are sexual, six neglect, and one emotional abuse.

254. Sigurdson, E. and M. Strang. 'The Role of a Rural Team
in Preventing Sexual Abuse of Children,' *Canadian
Family Physician*, 30 (Feb. 1984) 440-4
A team in rural Manitoba has identified 22 cases of
sexual abuse in the last 30 months. Methods of preventing such cases include educating adults and children
about normal and abnormal sexual behaviour. Early detection and intervention can be effected by establishing a registry of those at high risk for abusing their
children, and listening to children carefully to detect
signs of abuse early. When sexual abuse has already
occurred, its effects may be minimized with family
therapy sessions involving the victim and the offender.
   Community awareness, education and an interdisciplinary team have been shown to be effective in stopping
abuse and appear to have significant potential in preventing sexual abuse.

## Sexual Offenders

255. Brassard, M.R. and A.H. Tyler. 'Abuse in the Investigation of Intrafamilial Child Sexual Abuse,' *Child
Abuse and Neglect*, 8 (1984) 47-53

This paper examines the effects of current practice in the investigation and treatment of documented incest abusers on the offenders and families involved. Fifteen offenders attending the Utah Parents United group completed a questionnaire on the sequence of events in the investigation and prosecution of their cases and the concomitant results of the investigation on their job status, living and financial situations, family and social relationships, and media reporting of the abuse.

256. Dawson, R. 'Fathers Anonymous: A Group Treatment Program for Sexual Offenders,' *Journal* (Ontario Association of Children's Aid Societies), 26 (Nov. 1982) 1-6
As part of its beginning efforts to develop a comprehensive family sexual misuse treatment programme and in response to the treatment needs of fathers who have been sexually involved with their daughters, Oxford Family and Children's Services has for the past year, operated a group treatment programme for such fathers. The programme called Fathers Anonymous, although still in its developmental phase has achieved some modest success and may be of interest to practitioners providing treatment in the area of family sexual misuse.

257. Fowler, C., Burns, S.R. and J.E. Roehl. 'Counseling the Incest Offender,' *International Journal of Family Therapy*, 5 (Summer 1983) 92-7
The Center Against Sexual Assault in Phoenix, Arizona is currently treating 50 incest offenders in its Offender Group treatment prorgramme. The average age range is 31-45 years old, and 80 per cent were sexually or physically abused as children. These man have been found to be extremely self-centred, exhibit poor impulse control, and possess a strong denial of reality. The treatment programme includes several intake sessions to ascertain suitability of the offender to this type of therapeutic approach and a stated self-admission of at least the possibility of incestuous involvement. The offenders work in groups, as well as individual sessions.

258. Gilgun, J.F. and S. Gordon. 'Enlarging the Scope of Child Sexual Abuse Prevention to Include the Offender,' *Journal of Sex Education and Therapy*, 11 (Spring-Summer 1985) 46-52

This paper summarizes information about the offender
and outlines the components of a prevention programme.
These components include universal sex education which
fosters the basic values of the American democracy. The
development of self-esteem and a clear understanding of
what constitutes exploitative behaviour would be important parts of the programme. The prevention of child
sexual abuse requires the cooperation of many individuals from many walks of life: parents, educators, researchers, clinicians, school board members, and legislators. It would entail wide-spread social change.

259. Greenland, C. 'Dangerous Sexual Offender (DSO) Legislation in Canada, 1948-1977: An Experiment that Failed,'
*Canadian Journal of Criminology*, 26 (Jan. 1984) 1-12
The data presented here leaves little doubt that in its
twenty-nine years of existence, the DSO legislation has
conspicuously failed. It failed because the government
did not fulfill its promise to provide effective treatment facilities. It failed because 'dangerous sexual
offender' is a political and legal category and not a
clinical diagnosis. It failed because there are no
known treatments for socially determined conditions
such as psychopathy, mental retardation and sexual de-
viation. It failed because the courts, aided by psychiatrists, were demonstrably incapable of distinguishing
between offensive but relatively harmless pedophiles
and extremely dangerous habitual rapists.
    The most grievous failure of all has been that
neither the Parole Board nor the psychiatrists and
psychologists employed by it, have demonstrated a capacity to reliably predict the DSO's future capacity for
dangerous behaviour. The relatively high rate of parole
revocations, 38 per cent, indicates the crude state of
the art of clinical prediction. Using the same yard-
stick it can be reasonably assumed that this degree of
error works in both directions. We surmise that an
equal proportion of the DSO's who have never been re-
leased would not be dangerous if paroled.

260. Greer, J.G. and I.R. Stuart, eds. *The Sexual
Aggressor: Current Perspectives on Treatment*. New York,
N.Y.: Van Nostrand Reinhold, 1983
Greer and Stuart have collected papers representing the
state of the art and science on treating the offender.

The editors provide a practical and unified source of current technologies from the psychodynamically-oriented to behavioural therapy dealing with sexual agression. For the working professional in mental health services, the text focuses on contemporary management techniques and professional issues facing the sex offender therapist.

261. Groth, A.N., Hobson, W.F. and T.S. Gary. 'The Child Molester: Clinical Observations,' *Journal of Social Work and Human Sexuality*, 1 (Fall-Winter 1982) 129-44
An increasing amount of attention is being focused on the sexual victimization of children, yet no exact statistics exist in regard to this problem for a number of reasons: many such victimizations may go unreported or undetected, or the suspect may not be apprehended; or there may be insufficient evidence to go to court; or the offender is not convicted; or even if he is convicted his offense may fall under a number of different statutes which are not age-specific - in Massachusetts, for example, the sexual victimization of a child can be encompassed under 25 different statutes - and therefore it is impossible to retrieve the number of identified sexual offenses committed specifically against children. Nevertheless human service and criminal justice professionals are encountering more and more reported incidents of inter-generation sexual activity. The authors of this chapter are clinicians who have worked with identified sexual offenders against children in a variety of institutional and community-based settings.

262. Holmstrom, L.L. and A.W. Burgess. 'Sexual Behaviour of Assailants during Reported Rapes,' *Archives of Sexual Behaviour*, 9 (Oct. 1980) 427-39
This study reports on the forced sexual, excretory, and sadistic acts that occur during rape. The sample consisted of 115 adult, adolescent and child rape victims.

263. Tyler, A.H. and M.R. Brassard. 'Abuse in the Investigation and Treatment of Intrafamilial Child Sexual Abuse,' *Child Abuse and Neglect*, 8 (1) 1984, 47-53
This paper examines the effects of current practice in the investigation and treatment of documented incest abusers on the offenders and families involved. Fifteen offenders attending the Utah Parents United group

completed a questionnaire on the sequence of events in
the investigation and prosecution of their cases and
the concomitant results of the investigation on their
job status, living and financial situations, family and
social relationships, and media reporting of the
abuse. Results indicate that there is great variability
in the investigation and prosecution of incest cases
and the public announcement of abuse convictions. The
consequences of the abuse investigation are devastating
for offender and his family in terms of job loss; need
for public assistance; family disbandonment through removal of the offender, victim, or both from the family,
marital separation, and foster care for nonabused siblings; changes of residence, and the public announcement of the abuse in the media. Results also show that
offenders receive little, if any, social support from
family or friends. Changes in the current approach to
the investigation and prosecution of incest offenders
are proposed and include the following: 1) banning the
publication of convictions for child abuse; 2) stream-
lining the legal process so that it is consistent from
case to case; and 3) developing diversion programmes as
alternatives to prison for offenders. Suggested are
self-help, court-ordered therapeutic programmes, such
as Parents United, that are designed for the treatment
of families involved in child sexual abuse and incest.
The desired outcomes of such a diversion programme are
low offender recidivism, avoidance of the offender's
family being placed on welfare, less reliance on foster
care placement for the offender's children, involvement of the offender's family in moving toward reunion
when feasible, and the use of existing half-way houses
in lieu of incarceration when necessary.

Sibling Incest

264. Arndt, W.B. and B. Ladd. 'Sibling Incest Aversion as an
     Index of Oedipal Conflict,' *Journal of Personality
     Assessment*, 45 (Feb. 1981) 52-8
     Explores the possibility of using sibling incest aver-
     sion as an index of the Oedipal complex. Ninety stu-
     dents were asked to respond to a series of one hundred
     questions on brother-sister incest. Their responses
     were correlated with their guilt disposition, neurot-
     icism, extraversion, and sensitization-represssion.

Findings include: 1) males with sisters had a higher
aversion to incest; 2) low-aversion females tended to
express guiltfree attitudes towards sex; and 3) middle-
aversion females tended to have high sex guilt and dis-
play greater neuroticism. Concludes that sibling incest
aversion may be a valid index for the Oedipal complex.

265. Finkelhor, D. 'Sex among Siblings: A Survey of
Prevalence, Variety and Effects,' *Archives of Sexual
Behaviour*, 9 (June 1980) 171-93
Sex among siblings is a common experience. It cuts
across all ages, some are exploitative using force.
Females are much more vulnerable to exploitative
sibling sex.

266. de Young, M. 'Siblings of Oedipus: Brothers and Sisters of
Incest Victims,' *Child Welfare*, 60 (Sept.-Oct. 1981) 561-9
Although there is an extensive literature on the incest
victim and the incestuous parent and incest is recognized as a symptom of family pathology, few studies are
available on the siblings of the incest victim. The author widens the perspective on incest by investigating
the roles and problems of the siblings.

Surveys

267. Fritz, G.S., Stoll, K. and N.N. Wagner. 'A Comparison
of Males and Females Who Were Sexually Molested as
Children,' *Journal of Sex and Marital Therapy*, 7
(Spring 1981) 54-9
A 45-item questionnaire was administered to 952 college
students. The questionnaire covered the frequency, components, and adult consequences of child molestation in
a nonclinical population and provided the basis for
comparisons between molested females with and without
current sexual problems, and molested females vs molested males. The male molestation rate was 4.8 per
cent with a 3:2 ratio of hetero:homosexual molestation.
The female molestation rate was 7.7 per cent.

268. Schultz, L.G. and P. Jones. 'Sexual Abuse of Children:
Issues for Social Service and Health Professionals,'
*Child Welfare*, 62 (March-April 1983) 99-107
The results of a West Virginia Survey on the sexual
abuse of children challenge several popular myths about

child molestation. The authors point to the danger of
iatrogenic trauma and give intervention guidelines.

269. Selby, J.W., Calhoun, L.G., Jones, J.M. and L.
     Matthews. 'Families of Incest: A collation of clinical
     impressions,' *International Journal of Social Psychia-
     try*, 26 (Spring 1980) 7-16
     Surveyed 90 clinical workers regarding families in
     which father–daughter incest has occurred. Responses
     indicate that the incestuous relationship was typically
     not limited to one or two sexual encounters, but the
     relationship could become a stable part of family life.
     The sexual interactions appeared to parallel sexual
     practices in nonincestuous relationships. Daughters
     involved in incest were viewed as submissive, passive,
     fearful; the fathers were viewed as dominating, impul-
     sive, and using violence or threats to obtain the
     daughter's sexual cooperation. Mothers were viewed as
     weak and as failing to provide help for their
     daughters.

270. Tilelli, A., Turek, D. and A.C. Jaffe. 'Sexual Abuse of
     Children: Clinical Findings and Implications for
     Management,' *The New England Journal of Medicine*, Vol
     302 (Feb. 1980) 319-23
     To increase understanding of childhood sexual abuse,
     the authors reviewed the hospital records of 113 girls
     and 17 boys who were the victims of sexual offences.
     They were two to 16 years of age and seen in an 18-
     month period. Thirty had had medical or social prob-
     lems. Four had previously been raped. Children under
     eight years old were most likely to know the assailant,
     to be victims of recurrent sexual or physical abuse and
     to report crimes without intercourse. Incest victims
     were younger than other victims. Forty-three children
     had physical trauma. No pregnancies occurred, although
     diethylstilbestrol was not routinely used. Three girls
     had gonorrhea. Seventy-two patients were referred to
     hospital social services, and 41 to 17 other agencies.

Treatment of Children: Overview

271. Berliner, L. and D. Stevens. 'Clinical Issues in Child
     Sexual Abuse,' *Journal of Social Work and Human
     Security*, 1 (Fall–Winter 1982) 93-108

It is the author's observation that the values and generic skills of social work make it an obvious and competent profession to address the societal and individual problems of child sexual abuse. Yet social workers have often overlooked and minimized the extent and effects of this rampant form of child abuse. This paper examines the reluctance of social workers to become involved in treatment and prevention of this problem; describe the extent and dynamics of child sexual abuse; and recommend educational efforts so that social workers in the future are prepared to intervene more effectively on behalf of sexually abused children. These observations and recommendations are based on the authors' seven years of clinical experiences treating sexually abused children of all ages.

272. Carroll, E.A. and B. Gottlieb, eds. *Sexual Abuse: Therapeutic and Systems Consideration for the Child and Family.* Denver, Co.: The C. Henry Kempe Center, 1983 (1205 Oneida, Denver, Co. 80220)
Thirteen papers discuss system and treatment issues related to sexual abuse.

273. Children's Aid Society of Metropolitan Toronto. 'Child Sexual abuse.' *Our Children*, 20 (Summer 1983), Special Issue
In this issue treatment, investigation, and prosecution for sexual abuse is discussed.

274. Conte, J.R. 'Progress in Treating the Sexual Abuse of Children,' *Social Work*, 29 (May–June 1984) 258–63
Several conceptual obstacles to working effectively with cases of sexual abuse of children are discussed in this article. The author urges professionals to view sexual abuse in a larger context in which cultural values, social and political ideals, and economic conditions are seen as linked to the problem. He reviews progress in the development of professional interventions.

275. Conte, J.R. and L. Berliner. 'Sexual Abuse of Children: Implications for Practice,' *Social Casework*, 62 (Dec. 1981) 601–6
Descriptive data on sexually abused children confirm that most children are abused by members or acquaint-

ances of their own families. Social work services for
victims should include efforts to protect the child
from further abuse, and insure that the child, non-
abusing parent, and sex offender receive services.

276. Denham, P.L. 'Toward an understanding of child rape,'
     *Journal of Pastoral Care*, 36 (4), 1982, 235-45
     A discussion focuses on the role of chaplains who treat
     child rape victims in Philadelphia. Several differences
     between working with child and adult victims are noted.
     The anger and guilt expressed by children are more con-
     crete than those of adults, and children's perception
     of time is often undeveloped. In understanding the
     nature of the rape, children are handicapped by their
     limited life experiences. The family context in which
     children are seen can also complicate dealing with the
     rape.

277. Gelinas, D.J. 'Identification and Treatment of Incest
     Victims,' in E. Howell and M. Byers, eds. *Women and
     Mental Health*. New York, N.Y.: Basic Books, 1981
     The author discusses the treatment considerations re-
     lated to father-daughter or surrogate father-daughter
     incest.

278. Jones, J.G. 'Sexual Abuse of Children,' *American
     Journal of Diseases of Children*, 136 (Feb. 1982) 142-6
     Defines and discusses three types of child abuse: 1)
     pedophilia; 2) rape and other violent assaults; and 3)
     incest. General treatment for sexually abused children
     is outlined. The need for more research into child
     sexual abuse is noted.

279. Krieger, M.J., Rosenfeld, A.A., Gordon, A. and M.
     Bennett. 'Problems in the Psychotherapy of Children
     with Histories of Incest,' *American Journal of Psycho-
     therapy*, 34 No 1 (1980) 81-8
     Specific issues in the psychotherapy of children with
     histories of incest are identified. The first issue
     concerns the child's often seductive initial presenta-
     tion in therapy. Therapists must be cognizant of the
     meaning of the patients' presentation and the extreme
     need for therapeutic safety. The second issue addresses
     the more general difficulties and countertransference
     reactions experienced by therapists working with such

cases. The therapist must avoid allying with the child
solely as a victim. The therapist must work through his
outrage that a child has been molested so that he may
avoid blame-seeking.

280. MacFarlane, K. and J. Bulkley, 'Treating Child Sexual
Abuse: An Overview of Current Program Models,' *Journal
of Social Work and Human Sexuality*, 1 (Fall-Winter
1982) 69-92
The upsurge of interest in the problem of child sexual
abuse over the past five years has resulted in the
parallel growth of specialized treatment programs to
deal with this problem. In a 1976 survey, only 20
treatment programmes for sex offenders in the United
States could be identified. Of those, only one was
developed to deal exclusively with perpetrators of
child sexual abuse. Similarly, in 1978 the National
Center on Child Abuse and Neglect (NCCAN) estimated that
there were no more than a dozen programmes specifically designed to treat intrafamily child sexual abuse.
By 1981, NCCAN had identified more than 300 such programmes nationwide which contain specialized components
to deal with various aspects of this problem. Although
many of these programmes have benefitted from increased
federal and state funding, most survive on a year-to-
year basis with a combination of public and private
resources and client fees for service. Many are
struggling for survival in the face of rapidly increasing caseloads and diminishing public funds.
    This paper examines the range of child sexual abuse
programmes which provide treatment services in non-
residential, community settings. Specialized programmes
for abusers in prison or mental institutions are not
reviewed.

281. Mills, L., McCrae, K.N. and B. Gravenor. 'Child Abuse
in Winnipeg: Hospital and Community Together,' *Canada's
Mental Health*, 32 (June 1984) 10-15
A description of the child protection centre dealing
with sexually abused children at the Winnipeg
Children's Hospital.

282. Mengeot, S.W. 'The Impact of Cumulative Trauma in
Infancy: Some Treatment Techniques,' *Clinical Social
Work Journal*, 10 (4), 1982, 265-74

Children who have had major disruptions and traumas in
early developmental phases come to the attention of
child mental health specialists frequently. These
children present a complex and often puzzling picture
due to the early deficits. Without skilled intervention
further development will be hampered. Particular focus
is placed on the individuation process in the first two
years of life and its impact on early development of
affects and object relations. Theoretical considera-
tions and specific intervention techniques applying
this model are delineated in two case reports.

283. Stuart, I.R. and J.G. Greer, eds. *Victims of Sexual
Aggression: Treatment of Children, Women, and Men.* New
York, N.Y.: Van Nostrand Reinhold, 1984
This book covers a wide range of current therapies for
dealing with trauma caused by sexual assault. It gives
you a firm understanding of the psychological effects
suffered by victims and what can be done to mitigate
them. Each concept and technique has been tested in
actual practice and is explained by one of the leading
authorities in the field.

284. Summit, R.C. 'The Child Sexual Abuse Accommodation
Syndrome,' *Child Abuse and Neglect*, 7 (2) 1983, 177–93
Classifies the most typical reactions of children to
sexual abuse into a child abuse accommodation syndrome.
The syndrome is composed of two categories that define
basic childhood vulnerability and three categories that
are sequentially contingent on sexual assault: 1) secrecy; 2) helplessness; 3) entrapment and accommodation;
4) delayed, unconvincing disclosure; and 5) retraction.
The accommodation syndrome is proposed as a simple and
logical model for use by clinicians to improve understanding and acceptance of the child's position in the
complex and controversial dynamics of sexual victimization. Application of the syndrome tends to challenge
entrenched myths and prejudice. Providing credibility
and advocacy for the child within the home and the
courts and throughout the treatment process. The
child's coping strategies as analogues for subsequent
behavioural and psychological problems, including
implications for specific modalities of treatment, are
discussed.

285. Tucker-Adams, C. 'Early Treatment of Child Incest
     Victims,' *American Journal of Psychotherapy*, 38 (Oct.
     1984) 505-16
     The author relates in detail specific techniques and
     tools used in interviewing that augments the clini-
     cian's psychiatric understanding of the child incest
     victim.

286. Wachtel, A. and S.L. Speert. *Child Sexual Abuse: De-
     scriptions of Nine Program Approaches to Treatment.*
     Vancouver, B.C.: Social Planning and Research, United
     Way of the Lower Mainland, 1983
     Communities of all sizes face the challenge of develop-
     ing coordinated comprehensive treatment services for
     clients involved in child sexual abuse and incest. This
     report hopes to contribute towards the process of ser-
     vice planning by providing a compilation of nine illus-
     trative approaches. The descriptions are preceded by a
     discussion which emphasizes crucial questions about
     basic goals, underlying philosophy and treatment ap-
     proach. Decisions on these matters, together with what-
     ever structure of resource already exists in a particu-
     lar community, jointly influence the nature of the
     treatment response.

Treatment of Children

287. Anderson, C. and P. Mayes. 'Treating Family Sexual
     Abuse: The Humanistic Approach,' *Journal of Child Care*,
     1 (Sept. 1982) 31-46
     Presents an approach for treating the sexual abuse of
     children within the family context, based on the work
     of H. Giarretto (1978) but adapted to suit the local
     conditions in the city in which the present programme
     was developed. The approach involves a humanistic one
     toward individual counselling of all concerned in the
     family, followed by counselling of significant pairs (eg,
     mother and daughter). Victim groups are also important in
     this treatment strategy, in which detectives, social
     workers, prosecutors, and therapists work in cooperation
     in a common goal of removing the burden of guilt and
     damaged self-esteem that the assault has imposed on the
     child victim. The programme has been effective in helping
     more than 50 victims over a three-year period.

288. Becker, J.V., Skinner, L.J. and G.A. Abel. 'Treatment of a Four-Year-Old Victim of Incest,' *American Journal of Family Therapy*, 10 (Winter 1982), 41–6
A case study describing the use of behaviour techniques in the treatment of a four-year-old sexual assault victim is presented.

289. Carozza, P.M. and C.L. Heirsteiner. 'Young Female Incest Victims in Treatment: Stages of Growth with a Group Art Therapy Model,' *Clinical Social Work Journal*, 10 (Fall 1982) 165–75
This article describes a treatment model for female child incest victims combining art and group therapy. Five stages of growth are identified: gathering, self-disclosure, regression, reconstruction, and ending.

290. Dawson, R. 'The Use of Sexually Correct Dolls in Assessing Child Sexual Abuse,' *Journal* (Ontario Association of Children's Aid Societies) 28 (Feb. 1984) 9–16
Successful interviewing of children requires a knowledge of the develelopmental stages of childhood, skills in communicating with children, and an understanding of how the children differ from adults. It is these differences which make interviewing children a difficult undertaking. In comparison to adults, and especially in relation to the professional intervenor, children have a diminished vocabulary and general knowledge base. Their understanding of themselves, their world, the problem being discussed and the words used by the practitioner vary greatly according to their developmental status. Frequently children do not understand what it is adults are talking about. Some children may misinterpret or misunderstand adult words. Others may give adult words or concepts, their own frequently incorrect childhood meaning. Lengthy verbal face to face transactions of a complex and structured nature are not the normal mode of communication for children. Basic words, short sentences and simple concepts are necessary requirements for interviewing children.
   The article discusses the use of sexually correct dolls in working with sexually abused children.

291. ------. 'Therapeutic Intervention with Sexually Abused Children,' *Journal of Child Care*, 1 (6) 1984, 29–35

The sexual abuse of children has become an increasingly
salient issue for professionals in the field of child
care. The most critical aspect of providing help and
support to the abused child is understanding the
child's view of the problem. In this article, the principles of crisis intervention are outlined emphasizing
the need for professional sensitivity.

292. Delson, N. and M. Clark. 'Group Therapy with Sexually
Molested Children,' *Child Welfare*, 60 (March 1981)
175–82
Describes a play therapy group involving victims of
sexual abuse who were under twelve years of age
developed by the Humboldt County (California) Child
Sexual Abuse Treatment Program. The design and structure of the model play therapy group is presented and
the therapeutic techniques used are identified.

293. Friedemann, V.M. and M.K. Morgan. *Interviewing Sexual
Abuse Victims Using Anatomical Dolls*. Eugene, Or.:
Migima Designs, 1984 (P.O. Box 7006, Eugene, Or. 97401)
The Guidebook includes chapters on selecting dolls,
communication problems with children, pre-interviewing
preparation, establishing rapport, introducing dolls to
the child, interpreting what the child does with the
dolls, validating the child's information, ending the
interview, pre-trial preparation, legal issues using
dolls, training/practice exercises, and resources.

294. Janas, C. 'Family Violence and Child Sexual Abuse,'
*Medical Hypnoanalysis*, 4 (April 1983) 68–76
Discusses how analytical hypnotherapy may be incorporated into the cognitive, the catharsis, and the behavioural approaches when treating victims of family
violence or sexual abuse. The crisis reaction of a
victim to such a crime appears to have three phases:
impact, recoil, and reorganization. In the final phase,
the therapist can help the victim to avoid self-blame
and to overcome feelings of shame and failure. The author recommends that, when taking patients histories,
all patients be asked whether they have personally
suffered as the result of criminal activity. Perpetrators of child sexual abuse fall into two categories,
fixated and regressed. Children victimized by incest
tend to have a poor self-image and social skills,

unsatisfying social relationships, and they often act hostile or depressed.

295. Borgman, R. 'Problems of Sexually Abused Girls and their Treatment,' *Social Casework*, 65 (March 1984) 182-6
The problems and subsequent treatment of 16 institutionalized girls who had been sexually abused by adults were examined through social histories, interviews, psychological testing, and progress records. Of these, six were first abused at age 12 or older; the remainder were initially abused when under 11. For seven of the girls, the initial offender was the father; for three, the stepfather; and for six, another adult known to them. Seduction was involved in seven cases, coercion in five. The majority of mothers took direct action on hearing of the abuse, although nine were judged to have underreacted.

Women Sexually Abused as Children

296. Courtois, C.A. 'Studying and Counseling Women with Past Incest Experience,' *Victimology*, 5 (2-4) 1980, 322-34
The incest experiences of a volunteer sample of 31 women were investigated in a research setting using a structured interview methodology. Demographic characteristics of the sample, such as age, race, religion, education, marital status, parental status, and sibling rank are presented along with characteristics of the incest experience such as its frequency, duration, location, disclosure, and identity of the perpetrator. Ratings of the severity of the short-term and long-term aftereffects are presented.

297. Courtois, C.A. and D.L. Watts. 'Counselling Adult Women Who Experienced Incest in Childhood or Adolescence,' *Personnel and Guidance Journal*, 60 (Jan. 1982) 275-9
Provides a discussion for the counsellor on key aspects in the treatment of incest victims. Notes that the adult client may be reluctant to reveal childhood incest and that the counsellor must attempt to get the information in a calm and straightforward fashion. Recommends that following an incestuous disclosure, counsellor should find out the duration of the incestuous activity, age of onset, frequency, identity of the perpetrator, whether force was used, whether other

family members knew about it, and whether the act was
consensual or nonconsensual.

298. Deighton, J. and P. McPeek. 'Group Treatment: Adult
Victims of Childhood Sexual Abuse,' *Social Casework*, 66
(Sept. 1985) 403-10
A team of one male and one female therapist combines
family and group therapy to treat women who were incest
victims in childhood. Issues involved psychosexual dysfunction, parenting problems, and depression and suicidal ideation. Family-of-origin issues are emphasized.

299. Faria, G. and N. Belohlavek, 'Treating female adult
survivors of childhood incest,' *Social Casework*, 65
(Oct. 1984) 465-71
A discussion outlines the clinical issues and treatment
strategies involved in working with women who experienced incest in childhood. A working definition of incest is provided, along with indicators that can be
used to identify adult survivors. A frame of reference
that serves to guide the therapist's actions and under-
gird the course of treatment is described, and beginning therapeutic tasks and the overall goals of treatment are identified.

300. Gelinas, D.J. 'The Persistent Negative Effects of
Incest,' *Psychiatry*, 46 (Nov. 1983) 312-32
Discusses recent work with adults who were victims of
incest that has demonstrated that they show serious
negative effects arising from such sexual abuse. It is
suggested that no model has emerged to integrate the
various descriptions into a coherent, explanatory, and
heuristic framework to identify and explain the negative effects of incest on the victim. Victims of incest
tend to seek psychiatric treatment without disclosing
the early sexual abuse. Instead, they usually show a
characteristic 'disguised presentation.' It is proposed
that when the negative effects of incest are addressed
directly, treatment tends to be very successful. Seven
case histories are presented.

301. Golden, J. 'Incest: It's Time to Talk About it.'
*Canadian Woman Studies*, 4 (4) 1983, 82-4
A discussion about the importance of the victim of
incest discussing her experiences with a helper.

186 Annotated Bibliography

302. Gordy, P.L. 'Group Work that Supports Adults Victims of

186 Annotated Bibliography

302. Gordy, P.L. 'Group Work that Supports Adults Victims of Childhood Incest,' *Social Casework*, 64 (May 1983) 300-7
Discovery of common problems among women who suffered incest in childhood led to the development of group work treatment for them. The process made it possible for members to discuss topics such as guilt, low self-esteem, mistrust of men, and sexual dysfunction in beneficial ways.

303. Jehu, D. and M. Gazan. 'Psychosocial Adjustment of Women Who Were Sexually Victimized in Childhood or Adolescence,' *Canadian Journal of Community Mental Health*, 2 (Sept. 1983) 71-82
The interpersonal relationships of many victims are characterized by feelings of isolation, alienation, and difference from other people, together with much mistrust and insecurity. There is some conflict of evidence over the prevalence of hostile or fearful attitudes towards men. Some victims do appear to avoid a lasting relationship with a man and many engage in a series of more transient and casual relationships. Prostitution also seems to be associated with sexual victimization in childhood. Among victims there appear to be tendencies to oversexualize all relationships with men, to engage repeatedly in ill-matched and punitive partnerships, and to exhibit a fear of intimacy. The evidence is contradictory on the incidence of homosexuality among women victims.

304. Jehu, D., Gazan, M. and C. Klassen. 'Common Therapeutic Targets among Women Who Were Sexually abused in Childhood,' *Journal of Social Work and Human Sexuality*, 3 (Winter 1984-Spring 1985) 25-46
The range of psychological problems that are most likely to require therapeutic attention in programmes for women who were sexually abused in childhood are reviewed. In a series of 22 such women over three-quarters experienced low self-esteem, guilt, depression, and a variety of interpersonal difficulties. At least half these clients complained of some impairment in their sexual functioning. Therapeutic provision for suicide attempts and substance abuse is also very necessary with this client group.

305. Meiselman, K.C. 'Personality Characteristics of Incest
     History Psychotherapy Patients: A Research Note,'
     *Archives of Sexual Behavior*, 9 (June 1980) 195-7
     The MMPI records of 16 female psychotherapy patients
     who gave histories of incestuous experiences were com-
     pared with those of 16 patients who did not report in-
     cestuous experiences. The two groups were matched for
     age, education, ethnicity, and referring therapists.
     Mean profiles for the groups were very similar: how-
     ever, a prediction that patients with histories of in-
     cest would report more sexual problems than control
     patients was confirmed.

306. Romanik, R.L. and J. Goodwin. 'Adaptation to Pregnancy
     due to Childhood Sexual Abuse,' *Birth Psychology
     Bulletin*, 3 (July 1982) 143-50
     Describes five Anglo-American and Hispanic women (21-33
     years of age) who revealed a prior incest experience
     after being referred to psychiatric evaluation because
     of maladaptation to pregnancy. Two women were consider-
     ing having the baby adopted, two had sought to abort
     the pregnancy; and one was self-destructively alcoholic
     throughout the pregnancy. Three of the women were
     multiparous and had relinquished a total of seven pre-
     vious children to other caretakers. Brief psychotherapy
     during pregnancy focused on reworking the prior incest,
     particularly the relationship with the victim's
     parents. Although follow-up was limited, it seemed that
     all five women were able to maintain custody of the
     infant after giving birth.

307. Silbert, M.H. and A.M. Pines. 'Early Sexual Exploita-
     tion as an Influence in Prostitution,' *Social Work*, 28
     (July-Aug. 1983) 285-90
     The authors take a systematic approach to the question
     of whether street prostitutes were sexually exploited
     during their childhoods. A special instrument called
     the Sexual Assault Experiences Questionnaire was deve-
     loped for use in the study; it is seen to deal with 1)
     background information; 2) history of sexual assault
     during adulthood; 3) history of sexual exploitation
     during childhood; and 4) plans for the future. Study
     results document high levels of victimization of street

prostitutes before and following their entrance into
prostitution. Sixty per cent of the subjects are seen
to have been sexually exploited as juveniles by an
average of two males each; this mean includes as many
as eleven abusers. There is an urgent need to provide
services for juvenile victims of sexual exploitation,
the authors assert. Intervention services are needed 1)
at the time of the assault; 2) at the time the juvenile
runs away from home because of sexual exploitation; and
3) at the time a juvenile street prostitute undergoes
sexual abuse.

Miscellaneous (found after completion)

308. Alexander, P.C. 'A Systems Theory Conceptualization of
Incest,' *Family Process*, 24 (March 1985) 79–88
In this paper, father–daughter incest is examined from
the perspective of general systems theory. Three
characteristics of an open system – information exchange with the environment, negentropy, and dynamic
homeostasis – are described and examined with respect
to the functioning of incestuous families. Two case
studies of families with father–daughter incest illustrate the tendency of these families to be more characteristic of the 'closed' end of the continuum. The role
of the environment in the origin and maintenance of the
incestuous symptom is also examined. Implications for
treatment are presented within the context of this
theoretical perspective.

309. Finkelhor, D. and A. Browne. 'The Traumatic Impact of
Child Sexual Abuse: A Conceptualization,' *American
Journal of Orthopsychiatry*, 55 (Oct. 1985) 530–41
A framework is proposed for a more systematic understanding of the effects of child sexual abuse. Four
traumagenic dynamics – traumatic sexualization, betrayal, stigmatization, and powerlessness – are identified as the core of the psychological injury inflic-
ed by abuse. These dynamics can be used to make assessments of victimized children and to anticipate problems
to which these children may be vulnerable subsequently.
Implications for research are also considered.

310. White-Black, J. and C.M. Kline. 'Treating the Dissociative Process in Adult Victims of Childhood Incest,'
*Social Casework*, 66 (Sept. 1985) 394–402

Women victims of childhood incest are identified as
suffering from post-traumatic stress syndrome, with
dissociative processes. They can be helped to deal with
the problem in a long-term, open-ended group led by two
female therapists.

Resource Guide to Audio-Visual Materials

1. Department of Communications Media, University of
   Calgary, 2500 University Drive N.W., Calgary,
   Alberta T2N 1N4
   *Child Sexual Abuse: The Untold Secret*
   A 30-minute video and 16 mm film in which five adolescent girls describe the experience of being sexually
   abused by a father; the anxiety, guilt and fear; the
   relief on 'disclosure' and the struggle to build self-
   esteem. Presented by Peggy Mayes, MSW, and Carolyn
   Anderson, MSW, counsellors specializing in the treatment
   of family sexual abuse.

2. Ontario Ministry of Community and Social Services,
   Ontario Centre for the Prevention of Child Abuse, 21st
   Floor, 700 Bay Street, Ste. 2106, Toronto, Ont. M7A 1E9
   *Audio-Visual Resources on Child Abuse*
   All films available free on loan from: L.M. Media
   Marketing Services Ltd., 115 Torbay Road, Markham,
   Ontario L3R 2M9 (phone (416) 475-3750)

3. National Film Board of Canada, P.O. Box 6100, Montreal,
   Quebec H3C 3H5 (see also your local NFB office)
   a) *The Family Violence Film Collection*
   b) *Our Bodies Our Minds: Film, Video and Multi-Media
      Resources for Health Education*, 1984

4. Westwood Screen, 211 Watline Avenue, Mississauga,
   Ontario L4Z 1P3 (phone (416) 272-4300)
   *Child Sexual Abuse: What Your Children Should Know*
   A series of five films, hosted by actor Mike Farrell,
   includes a programme for parents and separate compo-
   nents for groupings K-3, Gr 4-7, Gr 7-12 and Senior High
   School. This series presents the facts, techniques and

information to help adults and children identify and avoid child sexual abuse. Each programme demonstrates ways that children can be taught safety and prevention skills that will make them less vulnerable.

5. Walt Disney Educational Media Company, 500 South Buena Vista Street, Burbank, California 91521
Walt Disney Educational Media announced two releases on the issue of child molestation:
*Child Molestation: Break the Silence* offers adults guidelines on how to identify symptoms in a child who has been sexually abused, how to respond, and most importantly, how to teach children to protect themselves. This film is designed for parents, teachers or anyone who supervises or spends time with children. (20 min)
*Now I Can Tell You My Secret* (Grades K-3) helps young children understand the difference between 'good touch' and 'bad touch,' tells them that they have a right to say 'No' to an adult, and encourages them to confide in a trusted adult if they have been abused or approached. (15 min)
Both films reassure viewers that child abuse can be prevented if all children learn they have a right to protect themselves. Each film includes a comprehensive teacher's guide with suggested discussion questions, role-playing activities, and an extensive bibliography for further research. They are available in 16mm film and videocassette format. A free two-week preview is offered in 16mm format only.

6. Children's Aid Society of Metropolitan Toronto, 2360 Dundas Street West, 3rd Floor, Toronto, Ontario M6P 4B2
*Sexual Abuse Treatment Project* (1984)
This film deals with the dynamics and treatment of child sexual abuse through interviews with the director of the Sexual Abuse Treatment Project and a client-mother in the programme.

7. Mobius International, 175 King Street East, Toronto, Ontario M5A 1J4
*No More Secrets*
This film, intended for children aged seven to 12, shows explicit, non-alarming scenes of sexual abuse within the family. Children demonstrate how to talk about incest to someone they trust, and how to say 'no' to intrusion.

8. Canadian Learning Co., 2229 Kingston Road, Suite 203,
   Scarborough, Ontario M1N 1T8
   Films on Child Abuse: *Boys Beware*; Child Abuse: *Don't
   Hide the Hurt*; Child Molestation: *A Crime Against
   Children*; Child Molestation: *When to Say No*.

9. Kinetic Film Enterprises Ltd., 781 Gerrard Street East,
   Toronto, Ontario M4M 1Y5 and 255 Delaware Avenue, Suite
   340, Buffalo, N.Y. 14202
   *Finding Out: Incest and Family Sexual Abuse*
   An examination of the most complex and least understood
   social taboo. Public awareness of the problem is only
   just beginning. In this film, Robin, a victim since age
   nine, talks about the devastating emotional effect of
   sexual abuse. Her mother tells how she dealt with the
   disclosure and subsequent break-up of her marriage and
   home. Other mothers describe their shocked reactions and
   their guilt at not having recognized the signs of sexual
   abuse.
   Also: *The Sixth Sense, A Chain to be Broken*

10. City Films Distribution Co. Ltd., 542 Gordon Baker Road,
    City of North York, Ontario M2H 3B4
    *If I Tell You a Secret (interviewing the sexually abused
    child)*
    It is important that those who must interview child-
    victims of sexual molestation be gentle and considerate
    but they must also be successful in eliciting the
    specific details which will hold up in court. This pro-
    gramme suggests techniques for interviewing.

11. Illusion Theater, Sexual Abuse Prevention Program, 304
    North Washington Avenue, Minneapolis, Minnesota 55405.
    Distributed by MTI Teleprograms, 3710 Commercial Avenue,
    Northbrook, Illinois 60062
    *Touch* (1983)
    Children 5-11, parents and professionals
    Film adaptation of Illusion Theater's educational theat-
    rical presentation 'Touch.' Presents a balanced approach
    to touch and sexual abuse, while helping viewers think
    of appropriate action to take if touch or other beha-
    viours become abusive or exploitive.

12. T.V. Ontario, Box 200, Stn O, Toronto, Ontario M4T 2T1
    Write for catalogue on videotapes available from T.V.
    Ontario on sexual abuse of children.

13. Les Nouvelles Cineastes, The New Film Group, 2340
    Lucerne, Suite 29, Montreal, Quebec H3R 2J8
    *Child Sexual Abuse: A Social-Historical Perspective*
    This videotape takes a look at the social factors that
    have influenced the sexual abuse of children. From the
    'Freudian cover-up' which excused the male abuser while
    pointing the finger at the victim, to the sexualized
    images of children in advertising today, our society has
    condoned and remained silent about childhood sexual
    abuse. Florence Rush, Louise Armstrong and others ex-
    pose the myths and misconceptions.
    *Child Sexual Abuse: Prevalance and Effects*
    Statistics on the prevalence of child sexual abuse, both
    in Canada from the Badgley Commission and in the United
    States from the work of Diana Russell, present a picture
    that people find hard to accept. This tape examines the
    reasons behind such high figures and looks at the ef-
    fects the abuse has on children. David Finkelhor dis-
    cusses the sexual traumatisation of abused children and
    Lucy Berliner talks about treatment strategies and
    setting realistic treatment targets.
    *Counselling the Sexual Abuse Survivor: A New Perspective*
    Many adults who seek counselling often do not present
    the symptoms of child sexual abuse. Many survivors have
    kept the secret, from themselves as well as from
    others. In this tape, Sandra Butler, therapist and
    author of *The Conspiracy of Silence* looks at issues and
    techniques for working with adult women who were sexual-
    ly abused in their childhood; and Linde Zingaro, of
    Vancouver's Alternative Shelter Society, talks of emo-
    tionally scarred teenagers.
       The videotapes are available in 3/4" V-Matic, 1/2"
    Beta or VHS cassette.

Addresses to Obtain Materials on Sexual Abuse of Children

Canada

Coordinator, National Victims Resource Centre, Ministry of
the Solicitor General, Ottawa, Ontario K1A OP8
   The database currently contains approximately 1,500 bib-
liographic records, over 200 service programme records,
detailed records of 150 victims research and demonstration
projects, and some 600 films and videotapes available in
Canada related to the victims topics.
   When you call us, a manual or computer search may be done
on your question, and a listing of material on your subject
is mailed out to you. If you wish to request a loan, simply
contact your library. All books, pamphlets, etc. have been
purchased by the Centre and are available through Inter-
library Loan. All films in the database come with a brief
description of their content and a list of films distribu-
tors. The NVRC does not purchase films. All victims projects
in the computer system have a contact person named on the
printout.

Independent Order of Foresters, 789 Don Mills Road, Don
Mills, Ontario M3C 1T5 and 100 Borden Avenue, Suite A,
Solana Beach, California 92075

Journal. Ontario Association of Children's Aid Societies,
2323 Yonge Street, Suite 505, Toronto, Ontario M4P 2C9

Metropolitan Chairman's Special Committee on Child Abuse,
443 Mount Pleasant Road, Second Floor, Toronto, Ontario M4S
2L8

National Clearinghouse on Family Violence, Health and Welfare Canada, Ottawa, Ontario K1A 1B5
   Publishes a newsletter Vis a vis.
   Central resource for sexual abuse of children information in Canada,
   Deals with the total area of family violence.

Ontario Centre for the Prevention of Child Abuse, 700 Bay Street, Suite 2106, Toronto, Ontario M7A 1E9
   Publishes a newsletter and has materials related to sexual abuse.

Social Planning and Research, United Way of the Lower Mainland, 1625 W. 8th Avenue, Vancouver, British Columbia V6J 1T9
   *Child Sexual Abuse Newsletter* and other publications.

United States

*Child Abuse & Neglect: The International Journal.* University of Colorado, School of Medicine, 1205 Oneida Street, Denver, Colorado 80220

Clearinghouse on Child Abuse and Neglect Information, P.O. Box 1182, Washington, D.C. 20013

Family Research Laboratory, University of New Hampshire, Durham, New Hampshire 03824. Dr. David Finkelhor, Director

C. Henry Kempe National Center for the Prevention and Treatment of Child Abuse and Neglect, 1205 Oneida Street, Denver, Colorado 80220

*Journal of Social Work and Human Sexuality.* Haworth Press, 75 Griswold Street, Binghampton, N.Y. 13904. David A. Shore, Editor

Learning Publications, P.O. Box 1326, Holmes Beach, Florida 33509

National Committee for the Prevention of Child Abuse, 332 South Michigan Avenue, Suite 1250, Chicago, Illinois 60604-4357

# Author Index

# THE CONTRIBUTORS

Chris Bagley is on the Faculty of Social Welfare, The University of Calgary, Alberta

Cheryl Boon is a Researcher at the University of Waterloo, Waterloo, Ontario

Ross Dawson is the Executive Director of the Family and Children's Services of Oxford County, Woodstock, Ontario

David Finkelhor is Associate Director, Family Violence Research Program, University of New Hampshire, Durham, New Hampshire, U.S.A.

Sol Gordon is the Director of the Institute for Family Research and Education, Syracuse, New York

Linda Halliday is a Sexual Abuse Consultant, Sexual Abuse Victims Anonymous, Campbell River, British Columbia

Benjamin Schlesinger is on the Faculty of Social Work, University of Toronto, Toronto, Ontario

Eric Sigurdson is Medical Officer of Health, Parkland, Manitoba

Malcolm Strang is a Supervisor with the Child and Family Services in Dauphin, Manitoba

Lada I. Tamarack is a member of the Healing Centre for Women in Ottawa, Ontario

Mary Wells is Co-ordinator, Support Services, The Metropolitan Chairman's Special Committee on Child Abuse, Toronto, Ontario

About the editor of the book

Ben Schlesinger was born in Berlin, Germany in 1928. After
living in Belgium, France, and Portugal, he arrived as a
refugee in Canada in 1942. He received his B.A. (Sociology)
from Sir George Williams College in Montreal in 1951, his
M.S.W. from the University of Toronto (Social Work) in 1953
and his Ph.D. from Cornell University in 1961 (Family
Relationships). He also was an intern in psychotherapy and
marriage counselling at the Merrill-Palmer Institute in
Detroit (1957-58). He worked for eight years as a social
worker with families and children.

Dr. Schlesinger has been on the staff of the Faculty of
Social Work at the Univeristy of Toronto since 1960. Pres-
ently he is a Professor, with special interests related to
the Canadian Family.

He is author and editor of twelve books: *The Multi-Problem
Family*, 3rd ed., *Poverty in Canada and the U.S.A.*, *The One-
Parent Family*, 4th ed., *The Jewish Family*, *Family Planning
in Canada: A Source Book*, *Sexual Behaviour in Canada*, *Sexual
Abuse of Children: A Resource Guide and Annotated Biblio-
graphy*, all published by the University of Toronto Press.
The book *Families: A Canadian Perspective and Families: Canada*
(also *Families: Canada*) was published by McGraw-Hill Ryerson,
*The Chatelaine Guide to Marriage* by Macmillan, and *One in
Ten: The Single Parent in Canada*, by the Guidance Centre,
Faculty of Education, University of Toronto. The latest book
is *The One-Parent Family in the 1980's* (University of Toronto
Press, 1985).

Dr. Schlesinger has a keen interest in international social
work and welcomed the opportunity of joining the Faculty of
'Aloka' the Advanced Study and Training Centre in Yelwal,
Mysore, India (1959-60). The 'Aloka' Centre, sponsored by the
World Assembly in Youth, provided leadership training for
young Asian and African leaders. During the academic year
1966-67, he was Visiting Professor of Social Work at the
University of the West Indies in Jamaica under the Canadian
External Aid Programme. During the 1971-72 academic year he
was Visiting Lecturer at the Univeristy of Western Australia
in Perth, Australia, in the Department of Social Work. During
the 1978-79 academic year he was Visiting Professor, Department of Sociology, University of Auckland, New Zealand.

He is the general editor of the 'Social Problems in Canada'
and the 'Canadian Social Patterns' series published by the
Guidance Centre, Faculty of Education, University of
Toronto. He is the author of six booklets in these series.